THE LEMMING FOLK

THE CONSERVATIONIST LEMMING

THE
LEMMING
FOLK

James Gibb Stuart

WILLIAM MACLELLAN

First Published 1980
An Embryo Book
Copyright © James Gibb Stuart 1980
ISBN 0 85335 237 2

ＥＭＢＲＹＯ *Books are published by*
William MacLellan (Embryo) Ltd
268 Bath Street
Glasgow G2 4JR

Drawings by
ANN MACGREGOR

Printed by C.M.S. 268 Bath Street, Glasgow G2 4JR

Contents

FOREWORD

When "The Mind Benders" appeared at the end of 1978, a colleague said, "O.k. You've told us all that's wrong. When do you start telling us how to put it right?"

Well latterly in this volume we get round to some proposals, — not a pontifical homily of personal wisdom, — but the resurrection, and the relevance to modern conditions, of other men's flashes of brilliant insight, — insight and brilliance which have somehow failed to make their justifiable impact upon our economic and political affairs because there were powerful vested interests which willed them into obscurity.

If a chemical monopoly has just laid down a billion pound installation to manufacture a new wonder drug for the pharmaceutical business, — that's a vested interest. And if some *kenspeckle* bio-chemist comes up with a discovery which makes the new drug obsolete before it has reached the market, he must not be unduly surprised to encounter the most infuriating obstacles in the development of his formula. He might also be advised to guard his laboratory against fire and bomb hazards, to stand well clear of electrified railway lines, and refrain from leaning out of skyscraper windows in the presence of unidentified strangers.

Milder, but no less frustrating discouragements might conceivably await the inspired innovator of the eternal electric light bulb, the self-sharpening razor blade, the perpetually charged dry battery, the unladderable pair of stocking tights, or the totally recyclable washing up liquid. What we are trying to

9

say, without getting ourselves into libel suits with bona fide chemical companies or honest-to-goodness manufacturers of household brand names, is that vested interests have a compulsive urge to protect their investments, and among the less scrupulous operators that urge has occasionally taken them outwith the law, — even into the realms of criminal skulduggery. The analogy has to be made, — and the point has to be established, — because as we wend our way through the antics and the errancies of the lemming folk, we finally come face to face with what might well prove to be the most malignant vested interest of all.

There is still a choice as between the open society and collectivism, freedom and bondage, — peace and war. But the options are narrowing, — and if by now the Soviets are marching, you can take it that *some* options are closed for ever.

An instant casualty of such a cataclysm would be the enforced suspension of those very qualities of reason and perception which are most needed to unravel and expose the sinister features of our social, political and economic system which periodically engulf us in Armageddon. We are long past believing nowadays that wars originate because of national antagonisms, — because the stolid Slavonic inhabitants of say Kharkov or Smolensk have any impulse to wipe out their opposite numbers in Minneapolis or Montreal or Manchester. In the present context for instance, global war will only have become a credible prospect because the new generation of Russian imperialists, with their vast and ever growing military establishment, are currently the appointed hatchet men for a sort of international mafia which is not beyond using both terror and revolution as deliberate instruments of policy.

Compulsive evidence in support of that mind-boggling assertion will emerge as the argument develops. The facts are no longer in dispute. It is merely a matter of breaking through the conspiracy of silence which prevents them from becoming general knowledge. As far back as 1972 that painstaking American academic, Professor Antony C. Sutton, with his authoritative researches into technical aid for the Soviet Union, had shown in exhaustive detail that ninety per cent of the sophisticated technology which went into the Russian war machine had been provided on the never-never by the United States and her NATO allies.

When Sutton publicised these findings in *National Suicide*, hardly a review or newspaper found them worthy of comment. Eight years later he and his researches are still under wraps, so that of the millions who elect and re-elect presidents and prime ministers, not one person in 10,000 will have been confronted by the gruesome paradox of a Western world threatened with nuclear catastrophe, which has yet been made to connive at its own destruction by the surreptitious furnishing of know-how, finance and military technology to the only credible aggressor.

In *The Lemming Folk* we try to plumb the depths of such paradoxes, to examine the motives and the mischiefs which inspired them, — and their capacity for jeopardising our national survival. As we do so we must be aware of that powerful vested interest which, even in an apparently free society, can still place subtle restraints upon the propagation of inconvenient knowledge.

Then courage to us all! We are about to pass through the gate which leads to the proscribed areas of the Garden. And inevitably we shall sample of the forbidden fruit.

"That . . .
The world should listen then,
As I am listening now"

From Shelley's Ode "To a Skylark"

12

CHAPTER ONE

¶ 1.   # The Lemming Urge

So who and what are the lemmings? Two-legged creatures they must be for sure, — since the author has no particular bent towards rodentology. Of course the most pronounced characteristic of the lemming species, that innate and still barely comprehended group instinct which has given their occasional mass migrations a morbid fascination, — is their capacity for self-destruction. Naturalists assure us that lemming swarms terminate with thousands rushing pell-mell to their deaths over a precipice or perishing in some considerable numbers by drowning in the sea.

The analogy is aptly and habitually used where human societies appear to have a similar death wish, and it needs no process of astute detection to deduce that the lemming folk of our title are about to be singled out and castigated as those elements in our midst who are working, either consciously or subconsciously, towards the enfeeblement and possible destruction of the social system which nurtured and sustains them.

But isn't it just a bit pompous and overbearing to sit in judgment upon a sizeable group of one's fellow citizens, announcing that *they* in particular are rocking the boat, letting the side down, deserting their posts, and generally opening up the gates to the enemy? After all, you might be pointing the finger at some dashed high-principled and well-meaning people, — people with means and experience and prestigious qualifications, and perhaps even an award or a decoration or two given in the service of the nation. *I mean, you surely wouldn't have the gall to characterise these people as lemmings?*

¶ 2.
THE FABIAN ETHIC — DISEASE OF CIVILISATION

Well that depends not so much upon breeding, background, position and accomplishments as it does upon the extent to which the subject has absorbed the Fabian ethic. Technological expertise, for instance, is absolutely no protection against the doctrines of defeatism and coercion. In fact a technologist is more likely to be led by the nose in this respect than the man who tends the cows down at the old home farm, — the latter, for all his lack of formal instruction and worldly poise, dwells closer to nature, and is therefore much less susceptible to the corrosive influences of a creed which etches itself more deeply into the pattern of civilised living. (Old Tom the cowman wants it to be known that he had always thought those high-falutin' ideas were bloody nonsense. The trouble was that when he spoke his mind, nobody wanted to listen.)

¶ 3.
INVERTING ESTABLISHED VALUES

The background to this cryptic comment anent the common sense of rustics, and the relative vulnerability of the technically gifted, is a breathtaking hypothesis, — progressively winning acceptance under sheer pressure of events, — that the Western democracies have in the last fifty years fallen prey to a false philosophy which, — because it provides no barriers against state collectivism, offers no safeguards for the preservation of individual freedoms, — might finally weaken and erode our liberal civilisation to the point where it would be no match, either militarily or psychologically, for the more militant ideologies of Eastern Europe and Asia. Detection and exposure of this misleading and pessimistic doctrine, along with a sharp reversal of the trends which it has set in motion, becomes therefore the most urgent task of our generation, — aye more urgent than reducing that golf handicap, or campaigning for round-the-clock T.V.

Debilitating social diseases are more often the affliction of the highly civilised, and this was to be no exception. It originated in Victorian London, perhaps at that time the most urbane and sophisticated corner of the globe. George Bernard Shaw was in at the inception. So also were Sidney and Beatrice Webb, that ingenious man-and-wife combination which in a lifetime of intrigue and permeation was to lay the groundwork for a pro-gramme of evolutionary change engineered so delicately and so modestly that only the politically astute would guess its ultimate objective.

Those early Fabians were Marxist revolutionaries thirty years before the Bolshevik conquest of Russia. The methods of Lenin and Stalin were not *their* methods. They abhorred the bloodshed and the purges, but covertly they endorsed the ends towards which it was all directed. And their own aims were very much in sympathy. In the England of their day they saw around them a social order that was securely based upon religion, patriotism, heredity, property, freedom of enterprise and the individual, – they resolved that in due course, and for their own purposes, they would turn all these beliefs and dearly held convictions totally upside down.

¶ 4.   CHANGING THE SIGNPOSTS

The story of how the Fabians came to dominate political and economic thinking in the great English-speaking democracies has been dealt with at some length in an earlier book "The Mind Benders", whose counter-revolutionary philosophy was welcomed by some, but vehemently rejected by others. If you have spent the best part of a lifetime travelling down a certain road, it is no easy thing to accept that you may have become disorientated at an early juncture, that the signposts which you so faithfully followed were deliberately falsified to confound you in error, and that you could conceivably be heading in the wrong direction. Confronted by such a maddening and frustrat-ing situation, many would rather forget where they had been

15

going, re-letter the signboards and opt for an entirely different destination.

The Fabians themselves do not take kindly to having their ideas derided by the unprivileged hoi-polloi, and they have their own means of ensuring that any form of reactive thinking is promptly discredited by the moulders of popular opinion. For fifty years now they have enjoyed such universal acceptance for their progressivist theories that even *they* might occasionally find it difficult to accept that there could be another point of view.

In this modern age, — which is the only one relevant to the present context, — their norms and their credos have been so widely disseminated that Fabianism can be more aptly regarded as a philosophy and an association of ideas than as a policy to be identified with a specific group of people. Through the British Labour Party, which it has controlled and directed from the beginning, it expressed itself in such sweeping collectivist ambitions as the nationalisation of production, distribution and exchange; in the subversion and dismemberment of Empire; in bureaucratic meddling and interference with the processes of invention and industry to such an extent that the benefits of improved technology are never fully realised.

WORLD WIDE COLLECTIVISM
¶ 5.   THE MENACE OF OUR TIME

In their defence it has also been argued that Fabian ideas have done much to alleviate the maldistribution of wealth, to improve the lot of the common man and to enhance the dignity of labour. Barring the fact that the original Fabians knew little about labour, except what they had mugged out of a textbook, — there is merit in these arguments, and had we been deliberating whilst such changes were taking place, we would have been obliged to measure the middle-term good against the longer-term evil.

But here we must remain strictly creatures of our day and generation, — must keep our eyes firmly fixed upon the menace of our time. That menace is world-wide collectivism, brought about by almost a century of Fabian infiltration into the governing bureaucracies of North America and Western Europe, — and now buttressed and pressurised by the military might of the Soviet Union, which has promised that in due course it will swallow us all into its totalitarian maw.

Nice thought, isn't it? Labour camps! Siberian salt mines! Political police! Thought police! KGB agents on the doorstep in the small hours of the morning! No Berlin wall, no frontier across which one might conceivably escape to freedom and a new life! No hope of change of any kind, because the conquest and the subsequent surrender will have been so complete that no haven of Western values could possibly survive!

¶ 6.   ESCAPISM ON TRANQUILLISERS

All right! even at this stage you are under no compulsion to go on reading, — any more than you might feel impelled to reach for a stirrup pump when you find the attic's on fire; or remonstrate with the bloke who's suddenly put a strangling grip on your windpipe. No doubt if things happened just as violently and as drastically as that, the adrenalin would flow swiftly and smoothly to the right places, and the instinct for self-preservation would produce a reaction and a riposte just as effective and as splendid as anything in our whole long Anglo-Saxon heritage.

Unfortunately the plot is not intended to unravel quite so abruptly. There is a conditioning process going on which means that you will probably be glued to the television whilst the attic is burning, and the family tyke, who tries to warn of the impending disaster, gets a kick in the tail because his excited yaps and growls are making it difficult to follow the dialogue. As for that bloke with lethal aspirations on your jugular vein, he won't show his hand till you're far gone on tranquillisers, and well on the way to complete anaesthesia.

17

LEMMUS BRITANNICUS

"Rule Britannia! . . . .
Britons never, never shall be slaves"

?

CHAPTER TWO

¶ 7.   **Lemmus Britannicus**

Still interested? Decided to stick around for a few pages more, to see who the lemmings are, — and whether the description measures up to the bloke at the office or the chap over the garden wall? Well it's particularly apt that we should think of things in that domestic setting, for the first of the types we're going to consider is the home-bred *lemmus britannicus* or *sleepy sickness* variety, — a social and political animal found in all stratas of British life, — and in a disturbing number of cases, found to be occupying positions of peculiar power.

¶ 8.   THE MYOPIC BREED

He's the fellow who blankly refuses to see any threat to our society at all, who reckons that if he does his little bit in his own regular groove, takes good care of Number One, and pays absolutely no attention to alarms and excursions off stage, the United Nations, the International Court of Justice and the Convention of Human Rights will ensure that no harm ever comes to him and his.

For this type of myopic lemming, all that stuff about *the price of freedom being eternal vigilance* is just so much outmoded rhetoric. Sophisticated wise guy that he is, he *knows* that if there was anything in these conspiracy or subversion scares, he would be hearing about it regularly on the telly. And when he reads his newspaper, — which he often does faithfully,

— he accepts both the fact and the comment with equal weight and judgment. If it's not true, he says, what would be the point of printing it? And when it comes to that hair-raising stuff about collectivism by stealth, totalitarian democracy, Marxism by the back door, he's mostly inclined to tell the kids to turn up the sound, so that he can hear what they're doing and saying on *Coronation Street* or Larry-what-you-call-'im's *Generation Game.* After a hard shift in the market place or on the factory floor, who the hell wants politics?

He likes *his* politics all neatly tied up in headlines and slogans, so that he can take them in at a glance. Without ever wanting to delve, he uncritically accepts the ongoing dialogue about the compassionate society, social justice, freedom from want, equal rights, non-discrimination by race, colour or creed.

Not so very long ago, this same easy-going type of citizen, — or his father or grandfather, — would be concerned with another type of politics, — the responsibilities of Empire, and the realities of world power. He was willing to get excited about a threat to the Indian Frontier, the security of the Persian Gulf states, or any impediment to navigation of the Suez Canal. Somehow the mood changed with the loss of the overseas possessions. The outside world with its harsh realities and its rivalries would *not* change. In fact it would steadily grow more brutal, more menacing than ever.

¶ 9.   OBSESSION WITH SOCIAL PROBLEMS

But this ordinary British citizen, abetted by his daily press and his elected politicians, had found a way of shutting it out of his consciousness.

It did not mean that there were less politics. Indeed there were now much more politics, but it had all developed into an obsession with social and domestic problems, — unemployment, sub-standard housing, sexual equality, rising crime, youthful delinquency, legalised abortion, the drug scene, trade union power, rising inflation, falling productivity, inner city decay, coloured immigration, population control, pollution of the enviroment, social security, the poverty trap and the pathos of

20

the one-parent family.

What a tangle! What a mass of problems! And the remarkable thing was that the more society became obsessed with them, the more professionals were engaged at inflation-proof salaries to cope with them at local and national levels, the less prospect there seemed that any of them would ever diminish or go away. So it was logical, wasn't it, that an increasing proportion of the national resources should go on being consumed by these problems? And in the circumstances, who would want to think about expanding our trade, building up our defences, or endeavouring to maintain our influence upon the world at large?

¶10.   OSTRICH IN A DANGEROUS WORLD

Opting out had become a British national characteristic during the nineteen-sixties, — and the myopic lemming got himself into phase very early on. When he was temporarily rocked out of his comfortable complacency by the oil crisis of 1973, — and the TV commentators and the politicians were finally forced to admit that we could do nothing about it because the abdications from Aden and Cyprus and Malta, and the successive cutbacks on our posts and bases overseas, had left us powerless in the hands of Middle Eastern oil sheikhs and international speculators, — he took on an air of quiet resignation, paid up for the fall in living standards, put on the telly, or went to bingo, — and tried to forget that there were elements beyond our native shores who had never heard of the Queensberry rules or the Geneva Convention.

The world was turning into a highly dangerous and uncertain place, — particularly for the British, who once had sailed the Seven Seas and spanned the five continents with good-natured tolerance and a sublime confidence in the *pax britannica*. The American strategic curtain, which had been promised as a cloak for the British withdrawal, showed signs of fraying at the edges, and as Western military and economic influences retreated, their places were taken by the new imperialists of Soviet Russia.

21

So the realities began to unfold. The cat was getting his whiskers out of the bag. All that process of rapid decolonisation, of ratting and scuttling from bases and strong points in the Far East and Middle East, in the Mediterranean and the Indian Ocean, was part of a plan to substitute one type of hegemony for another. Whilst it was happening, progressivist thought and teachings indicated that it was American hegemony which would be substituted, — and that it did not menace us. Now when the truth was known, that our place had been taken by one of the most ruthless totalitarian and collectivist forces the world had ever known, it seemed too late to do anything about it.

Thus the "in" thing became *"détente"*, disengagement, — agreement on arms levels and spheres of influence, — even though that condemned more than half the Universe to a slavery that apparently knew no ending. Our future and that of our children, our very existence as a nation, had passed under the control of a group of nameless military technicians, men who talked about megatonnage, degrees of overkill and first-strike capability. Nuclear arms had reached awesome, truly horrific proportions.

Was there ever a better reason, said the myopic lemming, for opting out, for shutting out the world and its cataclysmic posturings, for firmly closing one's eyes to the gloomy prospects and the gruesome probabilities, for adopting the low and passive posture, — for returning to the parish pump and its domestic wrangles, — for spending whatever time might be left to us in eternal and meaningless meandering?

Sober, cautions, — and above all reluctant, — that's him. Don't expect this little chap to lead the headlong rush over the precipice. Whatever he does, he'll want to do it slowly. He can be pushed, he can be prodded. He may in fact be dragged or even persuaded. But he'll wait till the others are going, and then he'll follow suit.

22

CHAPTER THREE

¶11.   # Lemmus Moderatus

Perhaps the nearest in mood and temperament to the myopic lemming is the moderate lemming, chiefly characterised by an almost obsessive desire for moderation in all things.

Now a day there was, — before the Marxist-Fabians took such a strong hold on our language, — when moderation was a considerable British virtue. In its non-political connotations, of course, the word can still be attributed the meanings which appear in the Concise Oxford Dictionary. Moderate performances in sports and academics, moderate tastes in eating and drinking habits, do not give the comrades an edge in the psycho-political contest, and are therefore permitted to retain a neutral status for the purposes of the Gradual Revolution.

¶12.   ## FEAR OF EXTREMISM

In almost all other aspects the moderate man who espouses moderate views and moderate things can find himself enticed on to a battleground which is not of his choosing.

The bait most commonly used to muddle and infuriate the lemmus moderatus is a strong suggestion of extremism. At the very hint of this, the most immoderate of all possible attitudes, his nostrils twitch and he goes off on a wild ramble which, if suitably supported among the rest of the swarm, can carry him right over the precipice. To achieve this dramatic effect it is not always necessary to define the attitudes and viewpoints wherein

23

ROBERT WELCH
Founder of the John Birch Society

the elements of extremism reside. Sometimes the use of the word itself is quite sufficient, whether it come from an Anglican cleric or the editor of "The Morning Star".

Moderates mumble a great deal about *consensus* and the need to find a compromise of the middle way. They are in their element with pendulums and other such symbolic digitalia, but the trouble is that they can never recover their bearings once the pointer has started to oscillate around a bit. Trying as always for that elusive median, they find themselves aiming at a moving target, and can often be detected clinging to an upper quadrant in the fond belief that they are occupying the bottom dead centre.

Angus Maude M.P., who is apparently not a lemming, once declared that there was no middle ground between common sense and lunacy, — and that very aptly illustrates the cruel dilemma in which the moderate finds himself as he endeavours to compromise and rationalise all the nastiness out of terror, revolution and communist collectivism.

In a recent report from America, William P. Hoar relates the story of a Ukrainian baptist who had been unwillingly conscripted into the Red Army. When his body was ultimately returned to his sorrowing family in a sealed coffin, they found that his face and head had been swollen out of all proportion by savage beatings. His eyes were gouged out, his tongue was torn from his mouth, and the fingers had been chopped from both his hands.

Not much moderation about that one! How does one find a compromise and a middle way by which to cope with sadistic savagery?

¶13.   STUDENT INTOLERANCE

On more than one occasion Sir Keith Joseph, a Conservative Cabinet minister, was both verbally and physically abused when he tried to set forth his views on monetary policy at several English universities. Joseph is not an arrogant or a discourteous man, his delivery is normally lucid and modestly presented, but those students had decided that his views were *extreme* because they themselves had been reared upon a diet of Marx and Keynes. They therefore bawled him out, invaded the platform, and effectively ensured that he should not have a hearing. They for their part claimed affiliation with socialist revolutionary movements which campaigned for abolition of the Monarchy, confiscation of wealth and property, establishment of a workers' republic aligned with the Soviet Union. This was not *extremism* because it was something in which *they* happened to believe.

Neither was it *extremism* to deny another man the opportunity of presenting his arguments. Only Voltaire was clown enough to insist that he would fight to the death so that the other fellow could have his say. The world and its morals have moved along since that period and the moderate has moved along with them. Amongst other things, he prefers the quiet life, and he just wishes people like Keith Joseph would not keep on doing and saying things which get these Left-wing chaps into such a fury.

¶14. MODERATION THAT PROTECTS MARXISM

The moderate himself could never be looked upon as a communist, — he has a fuddled notion that communism tends to the extreme. But one way or another, he can find himself spending quite a bit of his time defending communists against attack and exposure. It was *moderates* belonging to Americans for Democratic Action who thwarted Senator McCarthy's Committee of un-American Activities in its efforts to get subversives out of the U.S. Adminstration at the end of the Second World War. And in the British Labour Party, rent asunder by deep divergences of degree and ideology, it is the moderates who are fighting to hold the whole structure together, even if it means compromising every principle of democracy and national wellbeing.

In the Shakespearean classic *Romeo and Juliet* a fatally wounded Mercutio cried "A plague o' both your houses", and thereby provided the moderate lemming with a slogan and a moral stance from which to view the world's divergent ideologies and political systems. Being instinctively a creature of the centre, he looks on either side of him and professes in all sincerity to be both repelled and appalled by the excesses which he observes out there on the wings. He is not entirely untutored in the various -isms, to which as a good citizen he has from time to time given his interest and his attention. About the creatures of the Far Left he has never had any doubts or illusions. He abhors them for their intolerance and the inherent violence of their propagated doctrine. He knows about slave camps, breaches of human rights, and the awful corrupting influences of a System that turns men into unfeeling monsters. He will never ever vote to establish a Communist or extreme Left Wing government in office.

¶15.   LOADING THE PENDULUM

On the other side of the political spectrum he sees doctrines and practices that are equally pernicious and corrupting. Francoism in Spain, the military governments of Brazil and Argentine, the counter-revolutionary regime in Chile, all are calculated to set his sensitive nostrils twitching, and to inspire in him an involuntary revulsion that admits of neither qualification nor degree. He does not in fact feel inclined to look closely at any group or organisation whose views conflict with the consensus. It stands to reason that if it is not moderate, then it must be extreme, — and moderates abhor all forms of extremism.

This tendency of the *lemmus moderatus* blindly to exclude all theories, arguments and policies which carry the faintest whiff of extremism, has led to a cute little ploy of which the Marxist-Fabians can be justifiably, if circumspectly proud. Any research or propaganda which might seem to attack or erode the powerful positions which they have already attained within our society and governing bureaucracy is immediately singled out as the work of *agents provocateurs* or extremist paranoids, and summarily dismissed as such in the wide range of impressive publications which conform to the Fabian philosophical line. This is the point at which the politically aware should reserve judgment, and call for more information.

But the moderate lemming is not made of such stuff. With him first impressions are invariably the ones that matter, and if he sees any party or faction getting a derogatory editorial in the *New York Times* or the *Manchester Guardian,* that's good enough evidence for him that it can't be quite respectable, – and should be shunned by all reasonable, moderately minded people.

¶16.   SLAMMING THE BIRCHERS

An example of the skilful use of this *implied smear* technique was the propaganda fate meted out to the American John Birch Society in the nineteen-sixties. The John Birch was founded in 1958 by a Massachusetts candy maker called Robert Welch, who had become progressively disturbed by the Marxist collectivist influences which even then were beginning to show within the United States Government. In seeking a title for his society, he chose to immortalise the name of a certain Captain John Birch of the U.S. Army, who was put to death by Chinese Communists in the aftermath of the Japanese surrender, and whose life and motivation, thought Welch, had been sufficiently noble and uplifting to make him a symbol of anti-communist resistance.

For the business of the Birchers was anti-communism, – that was made quite clear at the beginning. Robert Welch and his society members started attacking the Marxist philosophy and ideology in all its many-sided proliferations, – and with particular reference to those areas where it had penetrated the American body politic. They proved adept at the game of counter-subversion, and in diagnosing those nuances of Marxist-Fabian teaching which that band of well-heeled élitist scare-crows would have preferred to keep to themselves. It was as though the Birchers had got hold of the textbook, and were interpreting the lessons almost as they were being delivered.

The Fabian Liberal Establishment closed ranks in earnest. From its vantage points in the bureaucracy, in the newspaper chains and in the other branches of the mass communications industry, it set out to give the Birchers and their works an image and a connotation which would shut them off from every decent clean-living American family. The prime target for this propaganda offensive was the founder himself. In 1954 Welch had undertaken an exhaustive study of the career and motives of General Dwight D. Eisenhower, as a result of which he came to a personal conclusion that the former Supreme Commander of the Allied Forces in Europe was a conscious instrument of Soviet intrigue and high policy. His findings were incorporated in a manuscript which for some years was circulated privately among his associates under the title of "The Politician", – and which was eventually published as a book in 1963.

¶ 17. EISENHOWER – AN AGENT OF THE LEFT?

To those many thousands of patriotic Americans who had proudly sported 'I like Ike' badges in the presidential campaigns of 1952 and 1956, the spectacle of the benign and affable ex-Supremo as an agent of the Communist conspiracy was one which they could only contemplate with incredulity and derision. Who? why? what? how? Welch just had to be a nut or a paranoic, – and with ninety per cent of the national press and radio networks saying likewise, you had to believe it if you wanted to keep your self respect and your social standing.

Here in Britain we had less cause to feel protective or sentimental about the obscure lieutenant-colonel who, in a short eighteen months, and without battle experience, was sky-rocketed to the top position in Allied Military Headquarters. To those who only knew him from a distance, he seemed too colourless and unexceptionable a character either to incite antagonism or inspire loyalty, and it was only towards the end of his first term as President of the United States that the benighted British saw some of the sinister implications which had prompted Robert Welch to write "The Politician". In the autumn of 1956, following some double-dealing by the American State Department over financing the Aswan Dam, Egypt's Colonel Nasser had retaliated against navigation in the Suez. Britain and France mounted a joint military operation to free the canal, and were in process of finalising the action when Eisenhower ordered the U.S. Navy to straddle our supply lines in the Mediterranean. It was perhaps one of the most inexplicable aberrations of American foreign policy towards her wartime allies, and combined with a threat of financial sanctions, it forced an ignominious Anglo-French withdrawal from an area which had relied upon their influence for its stability.

¶ 18.   MIDDLE EAST AND SOVIET POWER

The author recalls writing a long and respectful letter to Ike on that occasion, in which he pointed out the strategic dangers inherent in his policy. The facts were obvious enough, though at that time most British commentators assumed the U.S. President was eroding our position in the Middle East out of sheer ineptitude, or because of some undeclared motive of American self-interest. Robert Welch, — never a man for sweet talk or mollifying nuances, — just saw it all as part of a communist conspiracy. To those of us who since then have found many indications that such a conspiracy exists, the allegation that Eisenhower was implicated was something less than a mind-boggling sensation. Realists were aware that under his presidency, — as indeed under most of his successors, — the Russians would vastly increase their physical and their psychopolitical influence over the World's uncommitted peoples, and it was a matter of interpretation whether this could be put down to malicious intent or stupidity. In the words of a sardonic contemporary, if the house was burning down, it was more immediately important to put out the blaze than to consider whether it was started by arson or by accident.

But the prestigious journals and coast-to-coast broadcasters who set out to discredit the John Birch Society were not interested in putting out fires. Theirs was a killer instinct, and if they could do it by incineration, nothing was going to induce them to damp the flames. As with similar situations mentioned in this volume, they found many thousands of American lemmings to assist them in their purpose, — honest-to-goodness moderate-minded citizens who hated extremism in any shape or form, and who were willing to be quite immoderate in their persecution of any faction whose views were widely outwith the acceptable norm.

LEARNING THE TRUTH ABOUT
¶ 19.   COMMUNISM

The Birchers were castigated as racists, cranks, perverts and paranoids, peddlers in macabre melodrama, — alarmists, reputation destroyers, two-headed monsters who might secretly be devouring their own young. Liberal Republicans saw in their conservatism a bigger threat to their party and to the nation than the communist ideologies which they sought to oppose. Labour unions told their members that if the Birchers achieved their aim of getting the U.N. out of the U.S.A., the whole world would be wiped out by nuclear catastrophe. Moscow added its voice to the refrain by claiming that John Birch members had organised the murder of President Kennedy, and that it was financed by Texas oil millionaires who were intent on setting up a Fascist dictatorship. From time to time the Society was accused of fanning hatreds and divisiveness within the community, of allying itself with the Ku-Klux-Klan, of fomenting rumours about U.N. plans to train negro troops in Georgia for the internal conquest of the United States.

Meanwhile the J.B.S. was being investigated as a subversive organisation by a Californian State Senate Sub-committee on un-American Activities, which deliberated for two years before delivering its findings in June of 1963. The senators found no evidence that the John Birch was secret, Fascist, anti-semitic or un-American. Neither did they find the general membership to be "mentally unstable, crackpots, or hysterical about the threat of Communist subversion." Noting that there was an estimated total of 60,000 Birchers nationwide across the States, they believed the Society claimed so many adherents *"because it simply appeared to them to be the most effective, indeed the only organisation through which they could . . . . learn the truth about the Communist menace and then take some positive concerted action to prevent its spread."*

31

After that honourable vindication in a Californian state document, the John Birch was destined to survive and prosper. The facts which the senators had painstakingly unearthed for themselves were so much at variance with the hate propaganda peddled by the Fabian-controlled segments of the media that even the irrepressible Robert Welch seemed modest and restrained by contrast. Thenceforth the professionals would go more warily with their diatribes and their denunciations. The Birch Society had become a symbol of American conservatism, — of resistance to the Marxist-Fabian concepts which had taken a furtive stranglehold upon the Federal bureaucracy. Birchers became the leaders in tax reform, in criticisms of bloated government spending, in alerting the electorate to what their chosen representatives were doing after they packed their bags and joined the United States Congress. They started to publish regular reports upon how both congressmen and senators had voted on important national issues, and if a legislator ran on a programme of fiscal prudence, then went to Washington and supported a vast increase in the Federal Budget, his congressional district was likely to hear about it from a John Birch bulletin.

<h2 style="text-align:center">LEMMUS AMERICANUS —
¶ 20.   THE DANGEROUS ONE</h2>

The Society had moved on from the days when it was pilloried by the Establishment Press as a haven for the crank, the paranoid and the psychopathic anti-everything. It was living up to its reputation as a rallying point for all those who saw the danger of a collectivised America. Those most in contact with its ideals and its activities respected it deeply for its dedication and its patriotism. But still the memories and the effects of that old smear campaign lived on amongst those liberal souls for whom the whiff of extremism was enough on which to pass judgment and condemn. The *lemmus Americanus* was no better than his counterpart on this side of the Atlantic. He wasn't prejudiced, — but he was kinda slow in dropping his preconceived notions, and in the vast sprawling suburbs of middle-class America you'll still find folks who reckons these Birchers ain't quite nice to know.

All this at a time when American society was spawning the biggest proliferation of drug addicts, drop-outs and urban guerrillas in its history! It had needed the findings of a state sub-committee to confirm that patriotic zeal was not a subversive un-American activity.

¶21.   THE CONVERGING IDEOLOGIES

Confused by the apparently conflicting noises from both left and right, the moderate lemming therefore digs in his toes, and obstinately sticks to his middle ground. He *knows* that these are the two *extremes*. If they are not, then he is in danger of losing his reason. Communism, — that's an extreme. Fascism, — that's another extreme. Their adherents are bitter ideological enemies of each other. Put them in the same compound and they'll instinctively go for each other's throats.

The *lemmus moderatus* is not particularly good at analysing things back to first principles. He accepts that the Communists were left-wing socialists who came to power after the Bolshevik revolution of 1917. He is apparently less aware of the fact that the Fascisti were also left-wing socialists when Benito Mussolini led them to triumph in the Italy of the nineteen-twenties. Yet Fascism came to mean racism, repression, anti-semitism, reactionaryism, class-divisiveness, exploitation of the workers, — and a throwback to the conditions of the nineteenth century.

When he spoke to those students in the English universities, Sir Keith Joseph was dubbed a Fascist because he rejected Keynesian economics. Yet in Fascist Italy Mussolini was the first to admit that he had founded his own economic theories upon a study of John Maynard Keynes. And the corrupt Nazis of Hitler's Germany, who also began their careers as national socialists, were equally susceptible to the principles of state control and intervention which had initially been advanced in both Britain and America by the father of socialist economics.

Sir Oswald Mosley, leader of the British Union of Fascists, graduated to Fascism through the British Fabian Society, and John Strachey, regarded in his day as the chief theoretician of the Fabian movement, dabbled first with Fascism, then with Communism, before joining the Labour Party to achieve power as War Minister in Clem Attlee's first Socialist Government in 1945.

¶ 22.   THE MIDDLE GROUND

It's all a bit of a lark, isn't it? If Socialists, Fascists and Communists, — who persist in calling each other names, and indeed use these same names against all who cross or contradict them, — are actually fighting a phony war, with nothing but a thin wafer of ideological difference between them, for whose benefit are all their demonstrations, their hates and their post-urings? Can it all be for the confusion and eventual demoral-isation of the lemmings, who are expected to dash hither and thither before making that final headlong rush into the sea?

Lemmus moderatus, hearing that last suggestion, decides of course that *he* is not going to dash anywhere. It's scarcely the type of activity a moderate chap would favour. What he has to do now is sort out the whole bunch of them, — get things in the proper perspective. Maybe it doesn't matter all that much if all those extremists are part of the same extremism. Makes them easier to watch perhaps, if they're all out there on the same extended spur gibbering, shadow-boxing and posturing. A plague o' all their houses! Isn't it a relief to sit and watch them here, from the safety and certainty of the middle ground?

But who's this chappie who's edging along just that little bit to the left of centre? Says his name is Quintus Fabius, and he believes in a policy of gradualism. Well that's a comfort anyway, after all this heady extremism. One supposes that a 'gradualist' can belong to the middle ground, even if he does tend a bit to the left.

Nice steady dependable sort of chap anyway! Cultured and well-informed. Knows all about the various -isms, and can manage

34

to denigrate each one in turn without condemning it entirely. Come to think of it, perhaps that is the essential feature of the moderate, — an ability to examine all the viewpoints without being carried away by any.

¶ 23.   THE GRADUALISM OF QUINTUS FABIUS

This Fabius chappie seems just that shade different. *Lemmus moderatus* feels this is someone he can snuggle against without getting startled out of his wits. They get to talking of course, — and eventually Fabius admits that he too is for change, — meaningful irreversible change which will be all the more effective because it will come gradually. *Lemmus moderatus* declares that he has absolutely no objection to that, — provided it always takes place on a consensus of the middle ground. Whereupon the 'gradualist revolutionary', as he has now revealed himself to be, replies that there has never been any difficulty provided, as and when it's necessary, he's able to *move the middle ground* to wherever it suits him.

Move it to the extent perhaps, that instead of being a focus for the consensus, it has turned into a shifting slope potentially to trap the unwary? The ultimate condemnation of the moderate lemming is that some solutions in this ruthless world simply do not lend themselves to moderation. It was *moderate* policies in Northern Ireland which resulted in the deaths of Airey Neave and Lord Louis Mountbatten, as well as many sturdy young servicemen in between. *Moderate* treatment of murderers and violent criminals simply produces more killings and more violence. And if you want it in a sporting context, the football player who makes a *moderate* tackle when the other fellow's got the ball at his feet in the penalty area, is liable to get a knee in the thigh, or a studded boot planted in his groin.

Historically the Fabians themselves have always recognised that there would come a time when their *moderate* pose could be dropped entirely. The American Fabian-socialist Stuart Chase wrote in his *New Deal*, — a title subsequently borrowed by Franklyn D. Roosevelt, — that the new socialist regime of the future would enforce its statutes "by firing squad if necessary", and also in the United States, the Fabian-directed movement for Population Control has declared that if its aims cannot be achieved by voluntary means, they would contemplate the compulsory sterilisation of young women.

¶24.   GOOD COMMUNIST CAUSES

Norman Buchan, M.P., the long-serving member for Scotland's West Renfrewshire constituency, reportedly left the Communist fold after the *immoderate* things the Russians were doing to Hungarians at the time of the Budapest rising in 1956, but his switch to the British Labour Party brought him much more political influence than he would ever have enjoyed had he continued to rub shoulders with the comrades. And thenceforth the excesses, alleged or otherwise upon which he felt inclined to make public protest, – apartheid in South Africa, counter-revolution in Chile, anti-nuclear activity and participation in some of the campaigns to get the Americans out of Vietnam – were all good Communist causes, and strictly down the approved Soviet line. So the leopard does not really change his spots, – though he may from time to time get a convenient coat of camouflage. As to the moderation trap, – that is strictly for the lemmings.

As a final point of relevance, Rose L. Martin notes in her monumental work "Fabian Freeway" that when Sidney Webb and George Bernard Shaw, those arch-priests of Fabian gradualism, were in the USSR in 1932, their visit coincided with the deliberate campaign of famine-cum-terror by which Stalin wiped out some two to three million peasants in Crimea and the Ukraine as a prelude to his programme of farm collectivisation. None of these horrors was ever reported back in Britain, either through the literary giant G.B. Shaw, or the speeches and writings of the ebullient Sidney, who returned with his enthusiasms for the Bolshevik Revolution totally undiminished. His book *Soviet Socialism* was subsequently claimed by a colonel in the Russian army to have been ghost-written in the Soviet Foreign Office.

Sombre note for those fanatical devotees of the consensus!

If it should ever be allowed to happen here, have we any right to stand up before God and ask for ourselves a better fate than befell those peasants in the Ukraine? By that time of course the *lemmi moderati* will have long since gone on their migration, and been carried over the precipice.

LEMMUS MODERATUS
(The Myopic Breed)

This is the dangerous one!
Accepts all he sees on the telly,
Believes all he reads in his newspaper, —
And never gets involved.

CHAPTER FOUR

¶25.   # Lemmus Moralis

Just as standards of moderation have been traditionally regarded as considerable British virtues, so also have our *moral* strengths and attitudes been commended. As a nation we are inclined to take up a moral attitude upon almost anything, — whether it be the treatment of pit ponies or the inhumane slaughtering of livestock, — or the iniquities of child labour in the early days of the Industrial Revolution.

British moral opinion has served the world well, — as for instance when it forced the abolition of slavery throughout the British Empire, — or when diplomatic pressures eased the repressive conditions of many an Oriental princedom that came within our Imperial sway. We are used to having a high moral tone. In fact it is duly expected of us, — and in the days when British influence and ideas still meant something, what the British people thought on any particular issue could be of pressing importance to rulers and politicians from San Francisco all the way eastwards to Vladivostock.

It is still absolutely correct to have that high moral attitude. Standards can only be set by those who know better — and who have high standards themselves. But there is one serious drawback nowadays to the moral rectitude with which the British have tended to look down upon the rest of the world. The standards and the tone setters have changed. They are no longer Christian standards, — and there are sinister overtones in *the new morality* which force us to include a study of the *lemmus moralis* in this anthology of British lemming folk.

After the Second World War, Britain, in common with her Western allies, found that there was a new organisation which, among other things, had set itself up as the moral conscience of mankind. This was the United Nations, hurriedly formed in June of 1945 whilst the military men were still girding up for the final assault on Japan. World opinion knew little about the whole affair until afterwards, and the populations of Western Europe and the United States, still counting the cost of the Hitler war, would in any case have paid scant attention, except to give their uncritical approval to any organisation which would suceed in drawing the nations together, thus preventing a repeat performance of the holocaust they had recently endured.

That was essentially what the U.N. was intended to be, — a sort of parliament of all humanity, where disputes and differences could be aired in open forum, without resort to violence. Not only would it prevent conflict between nations, but as it matured, and its prestige and *moral* influence strengthened, it would also develop a procedure and a machinery for acting and mediating within nations, — in those cases where peoples or minorities were subject to injustice or repression.

¶ 26.   COMMUNIST INSPIRATION OF THE U.N.

A moral code was drawn up, embodying the basic freedoms, — freedom from want, freedom from fear, freedom from political and religious persecution. It all sounded unbelievably secure and morally uplifting, especially to peoples who had just known privation, persecution and destruction. There is no doubt that the new body was given wholehearted support and approval by the great mass of wondering and struggling mankind.

It was only years later that some doubts and misgivings began to arise. It was pointed out, for instance, in the days of the Committee of un-American activities, that Alger Hiss and Whittaker Chambers, two convicted American communists,

40

had figured prominently among the people responsible for drawing up the United Nations Charter. Hiss in particular was recognised as the leading member of the U.S. delegation in the formation of the organisation, and in this he was collaborating fully with known communists from the Soviet Union.

This then was the reality behind the world peace-keeping organisation which carried the hopes of millions. It had been dreamt up by communists, it had been drafted and manned by communists, and communists or communist sympathisers were prominent in formulating all of its policies. Many were deceived by the fact that the spot chosen for its headquarters was overlooking New York's East River, right in the heart of American Capitalism. There were reasons for that which will become obvious in the later stages of this volume.

¶27.
SIR ALEC HOME – STATESMAN WHO DARED TO CRITICISE

In its inception the U.N. functioned at two levels, – firstly through the Security Council, which was in effect a grouping of the wartime allies, – and secondly through the General Assembly, where representation was given equally to all the member states, whether they comprised vast sub-continents such as India, or tiny plenipotentiaries comprising a few hundred thousand inhabitants. Control of the General Assembly soon passed to a motley collection of Third World countries seemingly antagonistic to the larger power groupings, but the Western Allies were seen for many years to exercise effective control through their permanent grip on the Security Council.

This apparent majority control was however no more than a stalemate, as they were opposed on almost every essential point by Soviet Russia, who exercised a right of veto on any form of legislation which might undo some of the provisions that functioned in her favour. It was widely known, both to democratic peoples and their governments, that this stalemate existed, – and that the provisions were heavily loaded in favour of World Communism, but though individuals might express their scepticism, this was rarely if ever done by anyone in an official position of authority. The relationship between the U.N. and the elected governments of the Western World is similar to the relationship between the stoat and the rabbit.

Only one senior statesman in recent years has dared to speak out openly and critically about the United Nations. That was Sir Alec Home, for some years Foreign Secretary, and then latterly Prime Minister of Great Britain up to the autumn of 1964. Some misguided optimists might have felt then that Sir Alec's historic outburst was the beginning of a new era in our attitudes towards the U.N. Alas, that dramatic speech was a gallant, but never-to-be repeated indiscretion. One wonders why he should not have been impelled to repeat the performance, since justification for his criticisms was coming forth day by day. But subsequently unfortunate things started to happen to the career of the former belted earl.

He was attacked in the run-up to the 1964 General Election on a virulent BBC television series compered by the satirical David Frost, and there is no doubt that the influence of this bitter and abusive programme on public opinion was sufficient to deprive him of his premiership. The following year he also lost his leadership of the Conservative Party to the internationalist Edward Heath, — and though he made light of these setbacks, it seemed that he had been obliged to pay a heavy price in personal prestige and political influence for daring to cast aspersions upon some of the capers that took place within the glass-walled edifice overlooking New York's East River. Latterly he appeared in a grotesque role as chairman of an emasculated Bilderberg Group following the exposure, disgrace and resignation of Prince Bernhardt. Never a lemming, — even at his most subdued, — this gentlemanly elder statesman! But how did they manage to persuade him to wear the jester's cap?

¶ 28.   THE NEW MORALITY

So despite its monstrous birth, and the predatory and barefaced manner in which it has operated throughout the years as an instrument of Soviet policy, the U.N. has been able to carry out its edicts and its remonstrances almost without hindrance or criticism from the state departments and the chancelleries of the West. It has also succeeded in wrapping its doings and its utterances in a smug kind of moral authority which, because it has seldom been challenged at official levels, is now accepted as "world opinion", and becomes the standard for that new-type morality.

There are simple guidelines to *the new morality*, — though at first it can seem utterly mystifying in its double standards, and its failure on many occasions to recognise some of the elementary conditions of social justice. For instance, none of the brave new declarations about human rights were worth a jot when Russian tanks bulldozed their way through Budapest in 1956, — or a decade later, when Russian military power was again used to depose and imprison the Czechoslovakian Liberal Dubcek. In the West even practising communists were saddened and disillusioned by these events, but the muted response of the world organisation on both occasions got the message home to the oppressed peoples behind the Iron Curtain that there was no hope for their cause in that quarter.

¶ 29.   SUEZ AND HUNGARY

Yet the reaction had been ferocious when Britain and France moved back into the Suez Canal area in the autumn of 1956, — almost simultaneously with the Hungarian uprising. It was one of the criticisms levelled against the unfortunate Sir Anthony Eden in this country that his Suez adventure had distracted world attention from the agonies of Budapest, and had thereby destroyed the West's *moral* case for censure of the Russian aggression. Hindsight reveals this to have been a somewhat fatuous interpretation, — the Soviets and their covert collaborators already had sufficient of their own personnel manipulating the levers of power at the United Nations to see that the punishment of Hungary would continue unhindered by anything that might be done by the Security Council or the General Assembly.

Disquieting situations continued to arise all through the nineteen-sixties. Those who had given their qualified approval to the U.N. Organisation on the basis that it would preserve peace, had learned by this time that there would be no peace. But for this they blamed a variety of reasons, and not all of them were relevant to the matter in hand. It was impossible to understand what the U.N. was doing without going back to first principles, and to the agencies which had established it in the first place. Its conception had been dreamed up by hardline Russian communists and their *softline* Western allies, the Liberals and the Fabians, – and that last ditch rearguard, the *anti-anti-communists*, who stand ready as protectors and apologists for communist intrigue the whole world over.

Thus whatever else it did for the sake of diversion or distraction, the U.N.'s long-term policy would be for the furtherance of communist global strategy. So it has proved in the aftermath. All the great U.N. campaigns of the last twenty years have contributed to the growth of Russian hegemony. The dismantling of the British, French and Portuguese colonial empires, for instance! The rape of the Congo in 1961, – the ferocity with which they hunted down Moise Tshombe because he wanted to erect a viable free enterprise state in Katanga! The displacement of the French in Indo-China, first of all by an American military presence, and then finally and inevitably by repressive Communist regimes which taught the world something new in standards of twentieth century barbarity.

¶ 30.   UNANIMITY OF WORLD OPINION

All of this had been so successfully accomplished because it had been carried on under the cloak of that new morality which came to be known as "world opinion". Think hard about *world opinion,* and you will realise that in all the prominent cases where it has been brought to bear against a transgressor, it has been given the accolade of unanimity, which makes it artificial, since in real life human beings, and the nations which they compose, – are seldom unanimous about anything.

Yet world opinion, as promulgated through the U.N. General Assembly, has been unanimous about Franco's Spain, about Salazar's Portugal, about the counter-revolutionary goverment in Chile, about Ian Smith's Rhodesia, and about the everlasting bane of *apartheid* in South Africa. This has set the *moral* tone for world politics, – and all who aspire to become good citizens of a future world confederation, either subconsciously or deliberately, have set their standards by the cues and directives which emanate from the U.N. secretariat building in New York.

Following these cues and directives has led the faithful into some weird somersaults of mind and conscience. They found it quite easy to deplore and vilify Franco's Spain because of the General's long association with the Fascists and the Nazis. They were distinctly wary of Dr. Salazar in Portugal, for although the doctor was a very wise politician, and governed his country entirely without interference or meddling in other people's affairs, he was after all a dictator, – and good democrats are taught to beware of dictators, no matter how benevolent.

The bulk of the pathological moralists were quite ready to blow a series of fuses when Ian Smith opted for a continuation of white supremacy in Rhodesia, and they dutifully wept tears of indignation and sorrow when Dr. Allende's Marxist regime was brought to a violent end in Chile. But in the meantime there were some cross-currents and contradictions which gave pause to all but the ideologically committed. If the U.N. was so concerned about civil rights in Spain and Portugal and South Africa, for instance, why was it not equally concerned by Pandit Nehru's persectuion of the Naga hill tribes, or Communist China's obliteration of the Dalai Lama's ancient religious goverment in Tibet? Latterly also, when the fanatical Khmer Rouge were wiping out the populous city of Pnom Penh in Cambodia, the moral silence at the U.N. was so heavy that it could even be felt, and there were no special sessions of the General Assembly to consider what might be done for the thousands of refugees that the new Communist government of South Vietnam was driving to seek their salvation in leaky boats on the treacherous Gulf of Haiphong.

The solution was perfectly simple of course, – once you had embraced those first principles upon which the U.N.O. was originally founded. Vietnam and Cambodia, — and at that time Tibet, — were within the Russian sphere of influence, had already become part of the Soviet plan for world hegemony. They were therefore completely outwith the scope of human rights or civil liberties enactments, such as were proving temporarily useful for the dividing and the confusion of the still unconquered West. Countries and regions where the ideological struggle is over, and where the Marxist-Leninist philosophy reigns supreme, are technically in a state of *peace*, — and that *peace* cannot, and must not, be disturbed by the remonstrances of dissidents or the cries and wailings of reactionary elements in process of liquidation.

¶31.   SELECTIVE INDIGNATION

We therefore have now a reasonable understanding of the new morality, — and what it is intended to accomplish. Its function is to subvert, undermine or destroy those nation states, movements, parties and organisations which are seen to be resisting the progress of communism, — not just communism in its crude form, but also socialism and Fabianism and state collectivism, and all those other aspects of the gradual revolution which are intended to usher in the World Federalist Socialist State by a variety of routes and means.

This new morality, — or world opinion, — will thus concentrate its fervour and its idealism exclusively upon those aspects of predominately Western society where reaction to the communist code still persists. It will reserve its moral and humanistic indignation for those abuses and apparent abuses whose removal would advance the cause of World Communism. Equally so, it will feign to ignore no less serious abuses of human rights and civil liberties in those areas where investigation and moral approbium would react to the disadvantage of Soviet expansionism.

The result is that the new type moralist must be acutely sensitive, and at times highly selective, in deciding which brutalities and atrocities are to offend his moral conscience, — and which are to be studiously ignored. No use rending one's clothes and tearing a passion to tatters if, for instance, the Boukassa of the Central African Empire commits ritual murder on his juvenile subjects, or the new revolutionary goverment of Ethiopia conducts its business by firing squad! One can't make much psychopolitical mileage out of that!

But it's news if one of those South American right-wing dictatorships has to fire a few shots in suppression of a revolutionary riot. And it's *big* news if the police in apartheid-ridden South Africa can be tricked into maltreatment and abuse of one of their political prisoners, as happened in 1977 with the imprisonment and death of Steve Biko. One can feel free to become joyously and righteously indignant on occasions such as these. But don't let your indignation carry you to the point where you want to write or demonstrate about other unfortunates who for their views and their *dissidence* have been incarcerated long-term in Soviet hard-labour camps, — or have alternatively been drugged into perpetual zombiehood in Russia's psychiatric hospitals. Campaigns like these are scarcely helpful to the gradual revolution, and will be frowned upon by the Liberal Establishment here at home.

¶ 32.   BLACK PROPAGANDA

Observance of the new morality, — as practised by so many humanist churchmen and Marxist-inclined politicians in this country, — is now commonly called "selective indignation", and among initiates the rules and principles which guide it are generally well understood.

But in the mazy world of Marxist-Fabian propaganda, and in the incessant drive towards world hegemony, master strategists have had to evolve a refined technique which might most aptly be described as "synthetic indignation." This condition arises where the comrades and their fellow travellers become impatient whilst waiting for their ideological adversaries to commit some misdemeanour or ill-advised brutality which can be duly and righteously castigated before the bar of *world opinion*. They therefore proceed to mould and synthesise abuses and atrocities of their own invention.

47

Robert Moss, an investigative journalist who writes for "The Economist" and the "Daily Telegraph", refers to an entire department of the Russian KGB which is given over to "disinformation" or "black propaganda". This is once again an incursion into that quaint world of *nuspeak* or *double-think* first explored by George Orwell, – and in the current context it is taken to mean the deliberate manufacture of malicious falsehoods which, once propagated, can then be exploited for an ideological purpose.

"Black propaganda" is becoming one of the most effective weapons in the Soviet subversive armoury. The citizens of the still democratic West, who are of course the main targets of this psychopolitical weaponry, will eventually tumble to the double standards and the innuendos of "selective indignation", but they are often nonplussed and discomfited by a propaganda story which is either a monstrous caricature or one hundred per cent wicked "misinformation".

It is not to be assumed that the main outlet for this "black propaganda" is through the pages of *Pravda* or other inspired journals within the Iron Curtain countries. Wherever the Fabian ethic rules, the impulse to "create" or manipulate news is no less irresistible, – as when a roving photographer, sent to bring a horror story out of Rhodesia in the early days after U.D.I., filmed the recumbent Africans happily enjoying a lunchtime nap on the lawns of Cecil Square, and duly published his handiwork over a caption which indicated that Ian Smith "did not even bother to bury his dead".

¶ 33.   REVOLUTION IN SOUTH AMERICA

Stunts of this nature are generally most effective when fed to a public who have only a vague notion of the realities appertaining to any distant situation. For instance, South America being far outwith the ordinary Briton's personal experience, and being in any case inhabited by *dagoes* of unpredictable character and morals, it is apparently not too difficult for the liberal and subversive press to persuade a large proportion of the newspaper reading population that almost this entire sub-continent is crying out for liberation from brutal repressive governments. Several of the South American countries, such as Chile, Argentine and Brazil, have taken up strong anti-communist stances, and for this they come under perpetual attack by the world revolutionary movement, but all of them, both large and small, seem to have their localised guerrilla factions who disturb the peace, clash with the recognised forces of law and order, and generally prey on the community by holding up banks or kidnapping prominent citizens. Bandits they might be in the opinion of their fellow countrymen, but if they happen to be embarrassing a government which the internationalist conspirators wish to destroy, they can find themselves endowed with funds, motivation and an idealistic cause far outwith their original aspirations.

The recommended propaganda treatment in these cases is for all police and military retaliatory action to be labelled as mindless authoritarian violence, while the insurgents themselves get a very favourable press through some intrepid reporter who just happens to visit their jungle hide-out. Lacking any information to the contrary, the average *lemmus moralis* quickly comes to the conclusion that here is just another Fascist dictatorship over-ripe for a people's revolution, and if it should happen in due course that the Marxists mount sufficient forces for an eventual conquest, the incumbent government, which might have a long history of friendship and co-operation with the Western World, finds itself deserted in its hour of need.

A more brazen aspect of this propaganda technique is when the action takes place in our own streets and city squares, right close to home. Easy enough to attribute abnormal desires and sadistic impulses to a *dago* riot cop in a South American suburb, — *but our own local bobbies!* How to get charges of excessive violence and malicious brutality brought against a British police force which has been universally admired for its courtesy, its patience and its long-suffering equanimity in face of provocation?

Even so, thanks to the trend of criticism and denigration which the Fabians have introduced into all matters of law and order, that considerable feat has been accomplished in our time, so that policemen no longer can go about their appointed and often dangerous duties, secure in the confidence of a public whose lives and property they are there to protect.

¶34.　　　THE BLAIR PEACH INCIDENT

In Southall in the spring of 1979, during a violent political demonstration which caused injuries to ninety-seven members of the London Metropolitan Police, an unemployed schoolteacher called Blair Peach was struck down and subsequently found dead. In the court proceedings which ensued, thirty-five of the demonstrators were convicted of various offences ranging from deliberate obstruction to police assault, so it can be taken that those in the heart of the mêlée were in a situation where blows were being both given and received.

Blair Peach, whatever his attitude and degree of belligerence, had certainly not gone there to wave a white flag and plead for universal forbearance. The man who struck the fatal blow may not have known that he did so. But if he did know, he was obviously not prepared to talk about it. It was arguable that what had happened could only have occured in the heat of the moment and under considerable provocation. A messy business, out of which the police were entitled to receive some sympathy, both for their injuries and for their involvement in a fracas which was not of their choosing!

But this is not how it was seen by the Protest Movement. They initiated two campaigns, one to install the unfortunate Mr. Peach in the public memory as a revolutionary martyr; the other for the disbandment of the special police unit which had been monitoring and doubtless upsetting their plans.

No less could have been expected of them in the circumstances. They had taken a beating that day, they had been thwarted in their objective, and they had tragically lost an adherent. It would simply not have been true to form had they not endeavoured to squeeze the last ounce of political capital out of the publicity which they had gained at such a cost. But of course none of it would be for the benefit of their own

50

supporters, who are by way of being a cynical bunch, and seldom given to unnecessary sentiment.

The main shaft of their offensive would be aimed, as always, at that broad amorphous mass of humanity which wants to think well of everybody, and cannot conceive that anyone would practice deliberate deception in such matters. The affair of Blair Peach is not just a disjointed episode, with no interlinking or longer term significance. It is part of a pattern, — a closely woven pattern in a continuous design that will not leave the loom till the garment is fully fashioned.

¶ 35.   THE PATTERN OF DISRUPTION

Sometimes it is the dedicated and sinister KGB, scheming and plotting by direct espionage against the West's democratic institutions. Sometimes it is our own communications media, working up its own erratic and apparently disconnected campaigns to embarrass and discredit those who dare disrupt the march of collectivisation. Sometimes it is the ideological cranks, eagerly mopping up the "black propaganda" of the Moscow fabricators, and giving it prestige and credibility by the fervour and conviction with which they assert its malicious lies as gospel truth.

But none of them would get anywhere without the lemmings, — those ever-credulous creatures who *know* they've got their facts right because they heard it on the telly; who embrace the new morality with the same uncritical acquiescence as they might more worthily have bestowed upon the old; who are ready to believe that communism and Marxism have now acquired a human face, — just because they themselves have never seen a Soviet labour camp or the inside of a psychiatric clinic, — or have never been driven to an uncertain fate in a leaky sampan, as were thousands of the Vietnam boat people.

Yes, lemmings give communism its respectability. By their gratifying and too-willing acceptance of its unspeakable concepts, they encourage the comrades in their long, long haul towards that distant goal. The new morality is buoyed up and sustained by the lemming folk.

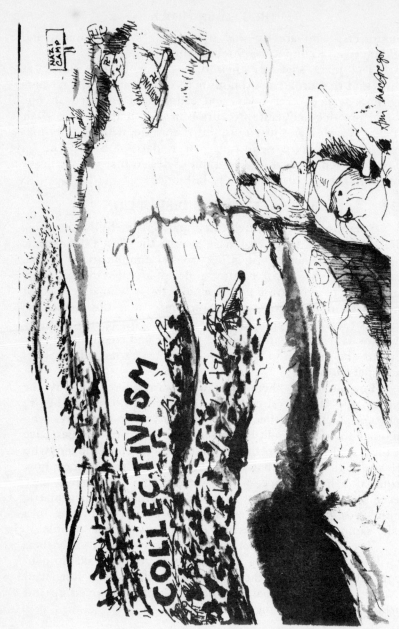

THE LOOK-BACK-TO-THE-LAST-WAR LEMMING

Still battling it out with the Nazis . . . whilst the Collectivist flood surges on.

CHAPTER FIVE

¶ 36.   # The Third World War

In that nostalgic autumn of 1939, whilst General Gamelin's *invincible* French Army was sitting fast behind its *impregnable* Maginot Line, and the British Expeditionary Force was busy digging trenches in Belgium in preparation for setpiece battles the following spring, there were just a few prescient but discredited strategists who had voiced their concern that the Allies appeared to be starting the Second World War where they had left off in the First, — with trench warfare and Flanders poppies all over again, artillery barrages, over the parapet at dawn, sticking it out in the mud, Armentieres, Ypres, and the cheerfulness and earthy humour of the British Tommy finally prevailing as of yore against the Teutonic stolidity of the Hun.

As we know in hindsight, these assumptions turned out to be disastrously wrong. The German *blitzkrieg* of May 1940 not only drove the B.E.F. back to the evacuation of Dunkirk, whilst grinding Gamelin's invincible French army into oblivion, it also swept away a whole anthology of preconceived notions about fortified fixed lines, static defence and muddling through. The only fortunate thing about that 1940 situation was that mercifully we were up against the same Teutonic adversary, and did not have to make a further series of adjustments for national character and psychology.

Now of course you realise what we're getting at. The above paragraphs would simply not be relevant unless we were going to follow up with some sombre warning against preparing to fight the Third World War with the same affiliations and mental attitudes which served us so well in the Second.

And immediately the defensive armour goes on. What was so wrong with our mental attitudes in that little lot then? We took a beating at Dunkirk, — and we came out of it still fighting. We stuck it out grimly while London was burning, — and planned for the day when we would give back ten times more than we received. We fought, and sang, and fought again, — and through it all remained a moderately cheerful and united people. Gained the admiration of the world, so we did! So what was wrong with that for attitude?

¶37.
PSYCHOPOLITICS AND THE ANTI NAZI LEAGUE

Well there is a school of thought which maintains that we should know more about the progress of this hypothetical Third World War than we ever did in advance about the Second, because, — they say, — without the formality of a declaration, or even the martial initiation of a trumpet blast, — hostilities have long since begun. They are referring of course to the secret psychopolitical war, — the cold war, — which the Soviets and their ideological allies have been waging against the Western democracies since before the days of the Nuremburg trials. Nothing new about that! Winston Churchill opened up the subject in his famous Fulton speech in 1947, and there's been constant reference ever since. In fact, taken in that context, it might be said that the whole of this volume on the Lemming Folk is dedicated to a study of the strategy and tactics of the Third World War. In which case, you may say, things are so vastly different that it seems inconceivable anyone could confuse our present situation with the honest-to-goodness up-and-at-them battle tactics of those two earlier encounters with the Hun.

No? Ever heard of the Anti-Nazi League? This is the militant body which organised the Southall demonstration in which Blair Peach was killed. That happened in April of 1979.

By September of the previous year the League had been able to claim 30,000 members, distributed throughout 250 branches, with additional support from public figures, stage personalities, pressmen, sportsmen and about thirty Labour M.P.'s.

The expressed purpose of the A.N.L.'s formation was to counter the resurgence of Nazism, which they saw as inherent in the philosophy and activities of the National Front, — another militant organisation which had had more than its due share of publicity in recent years.

One of the features which many people disliked about the National Front was its intolerance of Jews, coloured immigrants and socialist agitators. It had, however, achieved the status of a recognised political party, fulfilling its quota of candidates and constituency coverage to justify the award of a statutory amount of radio and television time. Under the law it also had a clear right to hold public meetings and explain its policies, in an unthreatened environment, to anyone who might be interested.

The Anti-Nazis showed their own respect for the democratic process by exhorting their members and sympathisers to harass the N.F. out of any form of peaceful public presentation, and through influence in the communications media, to "pull the plug" on any attempt which they might make to broadcast.

¶38.   WHY THE N.F. HAD PROSPERED

Let it be said here that the National Front had enjoyed a strong run of populist support in the days when there was persistent and surreptitious coloured immigration into Britain on a scale that was ignored by both the authorities and the principal political parties. People in the affected areas knew what was happening, and were frightened and disillusioned because no one in official circles would even accept that there was a problem. So they rallied to the N.F. because it was the only recognised political grouping which would give the subject an airing.

The publicised activities of the Race Relations Board did much to increase the Front's popular appeal, so also did the Fabian-Internationalist flavour of our foreign policy under

Tony Crosland and David Owen. For all their affiliations with a totalitarian legend of the recent past, the N.F. were robustly and unashamedly patriotic.

Folks who knew little about the gradual revolution and the projected New World Order were instinctively repelled by the mongrelisation of their race, and demoralised that none of their acknowledged political leaders seemed to care about the loss of national self-respect or the erosion of our traditions. There were many in those years who sincerely and thoughtfully believed that if their country was to survive as a sovereign nation, it could only be through a sudden and dramatic resurgence of the national spirit, such as the Front demanded in its public utterances.

Whether these dangers are now past is something which we will only know in time. Suffice it that the change in goverment attitude which took place even during the latter stages of the Callaghan administration removed from many minds the sense of national betrayal, and coincidentally deprived the N.F. of a large measure of its popular support. So its star was on the wane in any case. Not for the first time it had been established that the best way to counter an extremist movement was to eliminate some of its legitimate causes of protest.

But the Anti-Nazis were not content to see the National Front and its dogmas die a natural death. Having their own ideological base in the Socialist Workers Party, the Trotskyists and other left-wing revolutionary factions, they saw their initial success in rallying such a wide measure of respectable and non-sectarian support as an opportunity to weld the League into a permanent instrument of the class war. To this end they were actively promoting affiliated groups at the schools and universities, among women's guilds and through the trade unions. The common factor running through this broad muster of outlook, experience and opinion was to be a unanimity of action against the Nazis.

Against the Nazis! So who were the Nazis? Derivatively the National Socialists who followed Adolf Hitler into power in the Germany of the 1930's, and who supported him through twelve years of peace, war, triumph and disaster till his Third Reich collapsed around him in the ruins of the Berlin bunker. The Nazis in Germany have long since gone underground, died off, got democratised, or simply given up the unequal struggle. Whatever one might think of their wartime atrocities, and however one might sympathise with those who suffered permanent physical or psychological damage at their hands, they do not exist nowadays as a political force, – and pursuing them as such is like chasing the proverbial shadow.

¶ 39.　　　　LEMMINGS IN THE MEDIA

So why were 30,000 people, plus prominent sportsmen, theatrical personalities, writers and journalists, – and thirty Labour M.P.'s, – persuaded to think otherwise? For those who were ideologically committed it was of course an opportunity to pursue the revolutionary struggle through a new and previously untried medium. The organisers professed their delight at the number of young people whom the League had brought into politics for the first time, and obviously they would endeavour to retain that interest, whilst channelling it where possible into other socialist causes.

But what of the rest, – the broad spectrum of the uncommitted, – who were yet persudaded to give of their time and their substance in a cause which, far from ensuring their future against totalitarianism, was giving power and confidence and credibility to a band of ideologues, – themselves the forerunners of a tyranny for which Nazism was no more than a passing fashion? Did they realise that after more than half-a-century of Marxist-Fabian infiltration, the society which bred them was no longer rock-solid in its faith and its institutions, – that it could be schismatically divided by forcing people to take sides in such a ploy as the police-bashing exercise at Southall, or the efforts that were being made to thwart the law of the land by denying the National Front legitimate right of assembly and access to the media?

And what of the Fabians, that sly circumspect, élitist band of gradualist revolutionaries who in the latter decades of that half-century had insinuated their protégés and their like-thinking contemporaries into positions of influence and subtle power? What were *they* doing whilst their ideological comrades were planning the campaign in the streets? Well some of them, whose urge and whose natural attributes had guided them into the mass media business, were screening on television successive episodes of an American play called "Holocaust", which devoted itself to a study of Nazi persecution of the Jews during the Second World War.

This persecution, along with the death camps and the atrocities which accompanied it, was an established fact of history, and should neither be forgotten nor denied. But the timing of that television series, during the late summer of a year when the Anti-Nazi League had just got itself some 30,000 members, seemed too much of a coincidence to be fortuitous.

The reader will find that throughout this volume we address ourselves exclusively to problems of the present or the future. We may reach back in time to pick out incidents and precepts that have for us immediate or forward relevance, but we do not concern ourselves with matters that are over and done with.

The Nazi occupation of Europe is over and done with. So also are the miseries and the horrors that it engendered. What are not by any means contained or neutralised are the tentacles of that other totalitarian monster which has its maw in Moscow and its probing suckers ceaselessly searching and seeking around the capitals of Europe. Those opinion moulders who distract our attention from that horror of the present, whilst inviting us to wallow in anger and indignation over the admitted horrors of the past, may or may not know what they are doing. But if they *do* know, — and if they succeed in what they are doing, — let us assume that they have fixed for themselves a secure niche, or an escape route by which they will exit when society finally crumbles. They will start, like the others, in that headlong rush for the sea, but with an instinct for self-preservation foreign to the rest of the species, they will expect to drop out, double back and secure the pickings, without even getting their feet wet.

THE LEMMING FOLK

The rest of us could not all be so lucky. Lemmings! In this case the look-back-to-the-last-war type of lemming! It will take many hundreds of thousands of the little brown furry creatures, gnawing and nibbling at the foundations of our society, to bring it crashing down in ruins. The befuddled idealists who swelled the ranks of the Anti-Nazi League were but a few. But by playing out their anachronistic role as Nazi-baiters and Nazi haters they were handicapping themselves psychologically to such an extent that they might not recognise the real enemy when they saw him.

LEMMUS AMERICANUS

CHAPTER SIX

¶40. **The Conservationist Lemming**

As human life in its civilised state becomes more and more complex, as industry develops new processes, finds more and more chemicals to exploit, — and ultimately to discharge into our atmosphere or our rivers, — the subject of conservation is one that becomes of more and more pressing concern. Now that the word *oecology* has lost its Greek-sounding prefix, — and taken on a new meaning, — we find also that a cult has developed, not so much to increase the people's understanding of their environment, as to exploit those many vague and unspecified worries which are exacerbated by the stresses of modern living.

Nowadays when an academic or a recognised specialist takes on the mantle of an ecologist, he has almost guaranteed himself a dutiful and an attentive hearing. He has additionally ensured that for the time being at least, any spontaneous unfavourable reaction is likely to be moderate and muted. For who would dare to argue with an environmentalist or an ecologist? To do so is like to be arguing against health, the breathing of clean fresh air, the conquest of disease, the preservation of the species, the very dynamism that ensures the continuity of life itself. Who dares?

So what is conservation? It is something which appeals instantly to the countryman, the dweller in unspoiled and lonely places, the hill-walker, the mountaineer, the farmer and the stockbreeder, — everyone who has ever stood on a mountain top on a brisk clear morning and breathed God's good fresh air. It appeals to all who have ever thought deeply about the manner in which technological man is gobbling up the Earth's resources. It appeals to the thrifty, the economically-minded, the pinch-paring who save scraps of food, ends of string, trifles of this and that, who will never buy a new appliance if they can mend an old one. It appeals to all who have ever invoked the adage of "waste not, want not." It is the watchword of the wise and the frugal, the humble and the penitent, the scavengers and the cleaner-uppers, of all those who have had to live on modest means in a hard environment.

Conservation! Conservation of the land, and of the air we breathe, of the fish in the sea and of the minerals under the soil! There could surely be no more prudent policy for a consumer society than to conserve all its resources that are not being used, and of those that *are* used, to re-cycle them to the very limit of our ingenuity and capabilities. Where, oh where, could there ever be subversion in this? Should we not rather be diverting our attention towards the wasters and the gobblers, the advocates of rapid erosion and high depreciation, the land-grabbers, the steel-and-concrete jungle builders, the mining sharks who devastate but do not rehabilitate? Is it possible to be a conservationist, — and a lemming as well?

¶41.
THE ATTACK ON OUR ENERGY SOURCES

In his "Energy or Extinction", published July 1977, Sir Frederick Hoyle, a distinguished British astronomer, points to the dangers of a desire for conservation being allowed to subdue all other considerations. In a survey encompassing the presently available sources of world energy, such as the Middle East oil-fields, eastwards to the U.S.S.R. and westwards through North Africa and across the Atlantic to Mexico and Texas, Sir Fred indicates how our lifelines to these sources are becoming more vulnerable as time goes by, — and declares that, with the working out and exhaustion of so many of the proven reserves, the only viable alternative for the West to use in the future is nuclear power. It is, he affirms with satisfaction, a development in which Britain was foremost, and in which the West as a whole has a firm and unassailable technical lead.

What can be more encouraging than that? We may be in a perpetual state of decline, — as dutifully noted for his Russian readers by the London correspondent of *Pravda* during the winter of 1978-79. But if, as Sir Fred maintains, we are tops in nuclear energy technology, then we might just one day reverse that decline, and preserve a society that can be handed on to our children yet unborn.

So where's the catch? Well it appears that we have an anti-nuclear protest movement which not only urges us to do away with our nuclear armoury, but also wants to dispense with the peaceful advantages of nuclear energy as well. One of the organisations which is prominent in this campaign is *"Friends of the Earth"*, an erstwhile little known body which made the headlines in 1976 when one of its British representatives, a certain Amory B. Lovins, a young man lacking degrees or technical qualifications, was allowed to put over in the prestigious American journal *Foreign Affairs*, a treatise on what he called "soft energy" techniques, using wind power and tides and solar panels, as opposed to what he called the "hard" technologies of coal and oil and nuclear fission. This was seized upon by the environmentalists and conservationists as a pattern for the future, — and used to bolster up their earlier claims that we are rapidly running out of fossil fuels such as oil and gas, and would have to find alternative sources which were self-replenishing, and not subject to depletion.

Astronomer Hoyle takes the point about the limited life of current oil and gas supplies, and reckons that even our coal deposits may be worked out when we are eighty years further on. But when he discusses the availability of uranium and thorium, which are the essential raw materials of nuclear fission, he talks in terms of millenia rather than of decades. He is also quite blunt about many of the conservationist ploys and political protest movements which have inhibited industrial and technological progress during the post-war years. Gas and oil supplies are limited, he concedes, but a major objective of Soviet Russia's grand global strategy is to try and collar for her own use and advantage such supplies as do remain. To this end she makes her principal play in two areas, — the Middle East and Southern Africa, — firstly to lay hands on the Arab oilfields, and secondly to capture the Cape route, without control of which the Western World would be split in two.

¶42.   NUCLEAR TREACHERY

Is Sir Fred Hoyle a nut, or a paranoic or something? Do the rest of us, with a modicum of worldly experience or general knowledge, find it so very difficult to see what he is driving at? His book "Energy and Extinction" has not been so widely read as for instance the annals of Elvis Presley, or the night life of Marilyn Monroe, and even after the energy crisis of 1979, one doubts whether it will be allowed any wider publicity through the reviewing networks, since it says things which are unmentionable in certain influential quarters of the Fabian Establishment.

As has already been indicated, it is always wise to listen to those experts who advise on the husbanding of our resources. And it is only commonsense, while developing the existing sources, to keep looking around for others. We must accept that what is absurd and impracticable today may become a viable propostion in the future. But what Sir Fred Hoyle is saying is that the anti-nuclear conservationist is looking at the problem with either a split mind or blinkers.

It may be a natural reaction at this stage to wish that atomic fission had never been discovered, — that the Yanks had never produced the bombs which destroyed Nagasaki and Hiroshima. But these things have happened, they cannot be undone, — and in the meantime, thanks to the ideologically motivated efforts of traitors within our governmental and defence establishments, — and the protection which they have enjoyed from the Fabian élite within our British and American bureaucracies, — every nuclear secret that we ever possessed has been passed on with tender care to the Russians, who have indicated again and again that they mean to destroy us.

¶43.   A TRANSPARENT RUSE

It was reported that *Friends of the Earth* and other anti-nuclear groups were frankly astonished to hear that Astronomer Hoyle had categorised them as communist dupes. *Friends of the Earth* may not be a Communist Front organisation, but it is known that communists operate comfortably within its ranks, and its schizophrenic approach to the uses of nuclear energy might ·be more generally acceptable if we knew that similar movements were being given publicity and encouragement on the other side of the Iron Curtain. Are the   Soviets being persuaded to go slow on their nuclear developments for ecological reasons? If they were, it might be possible to have a joining of hands and the unity of a common purpose among all the world's peoples who have a revulsion against being incinerated. It may be that the Russians have problems, — but we can bet the proverbial bottom dollar that they are technological problems, — and whilst they are sorting them out, it makes good sense to disrupt the nuclear programmes of their rivals in Britain and America, who, according to Sir Fred Hoyle, have amassed a powerful nuclear technology which Moscow both envies and fears.

It is in this process of disruption that the Conservationist Lemming plays a crucial and indispensable part.

¶44.   CONSERVATION OR SUBVERSION?

It had better be emphasised again that conservation in itself is not a symptom of subversion. Quite the contrary, in fact! Wherever resources or materials assume finite dimensions, it becomes an urgent national necessity to make the best use of what we have. And those who conserve, re-cycle, and find more economical methods of using our existing resources are entitled to receive the best rewards that a grateful community can offer. But on the current evidence, conservation as an ideology, as a be-all and end-all, as a style of life and a dedicated goal, is something that has to be carefully watched.

The subversive, searching for a means to widen his appeal, very often seizes upon an issue which evokes massive sympathy and nation-wide interest. For instance, towards the end of 1978, the Scottish people heard a great deal about an organisation called *Greenpeace*, which was co-ordinating opposition to a mass extermination of grey seal pups on the Orkney Islands. Their venture caught the imagination of many of the younger and more sentimental members of the community, the nature and animal lovers, the school kids and the grandmothers. The official reason for "culling" the pups was that an escalating seal population would decimate the local fish breeding grounds, and endanger livelihoods amongst the fishing community. *Greenpeace* and its small army of supporters so organised themselves, and so rallied national opinion on their side, that enentually the "cull" was called off, and local interests were left to deal with the surplus seal population on their own.

So far, so good! Even hardened cynics who seldom saw a seal breathed a sigh of relief that the highly publicised slaughter had been averted. And David McTaggart, the man who masterminded the *Greenpeace* operation, made the headlines as he talked about his organisation and its activities. Apparently his first *conservationist* exploit was when he frustrated a French attempt to detonate a nuclear device at the Muroroa Atoll in the South Pacific, and subsequently he was involved with a group of Canadian protesters who in 1970 tried to thwart an American nuclear test on the Aleutians. More recently and closer to home, he and his colleagues had joined in the objections to building the nuclear plant at Windscale in the North of England, and there were *Greenpeace* representatives among the sit-in demonstrators who disrupted ground clearing operations for the other new nuclear site at Torness in East Lothian.

¶45.   THE IDEALS OF S.C.R.A.M.

Torness, about five miles from the Scottish town of Dunbar, had been protested about, camped upon and picketed persistently in the months before work began. In May of 1978 it witnessed a two-day occupation by about 2,000 people representing various anti-nuclear groups. These were not local people, farmers, lovers of the countryside, frequenters of bird sanctuaries and of the quiet lonely places, such as would instinctively resent the intrusion of bulldozers and mechanical handling plant into their peaceful environment. In fact the noise that they brought with them was even less musical to the civilised ear than the din of the tractors and mechanical shovels they came to supplant. Many of them were semi-professional protesters, from all corners of Britain, and from as far away as Central Europe, — able and willing, as duty called, to hump their rucksacks and their guitars, stage their demo. and then be gone. An American writer notes for instance that during violent demonstrations against the Brokdorf Nuclear Station in West Germany, an appreciable number of the protesters were financed and instructed from East Berlin.

Technically the May '78 sit-in at Torness was under the control of S.C.R.A.M. (Scottish Campaign to Resist Atomic Menace). Their spokesman, a Mr. Rob Edwards, said that he and his associates were prepared to take all non-violent steps to prevent construction of the nuclear station. Their stand was "in defence of health and safety"; for "future generations and all living creatures on this planet."

¶46.   ECOLOGY AND SURRENDER

Mr. Edwards of course had his point. We all want health and safety, — and we all want a future in which it will be pleasant and eminently possible for living creatures to go on existing on this planet. But as free men, — not in bondage!

The basic tenet of this volume is that while most of us are going our innocent ways, there are powerful influences about who are intent on world domination, — and who will surely achieve that domination if we surrender to them in the battle for resources. According to the eminent Sir Fred Hoyle, the one credible energy source of which we still have unlimited supplies at our disposal, — and in which moreover we still appear to have an impressive technological lead over the Soviets, — is in the development of nuclear power.

In the nineteen fifties and sixties the main target of the anti-nuclear protest movement in this country was the British nuclear deterrent. For many years Easter in Merry England was signalled by the gathering of the Aldermaston marchers, and when the Americans built a nuclear base in the Clyde estuary to accommodate their Polaris submarines, much of the action moved up to the West of Scotland, where a section of the Scottish National Party joined in the agitation, — though *their* particular complaint seemed to be less against the deterrent than about the fact that it had been based on Scottish soil.

For those who may still doubt that there is anything subversive in the drive to dispossess us of the sophisticated weapon which, in its absence, would leave us totally at the mercy of the World's most implacable aggressor, there may be interest in the following anecdote.

¶47.   JUDITH HART AND THE COMMITTEE OF 100

During those earlier years, before the arrival of S.C.R.A.M. and Friends of the Earth and Greenpeace, the gathering call for the Protest Movement was sounded by the Campaign for Nuclear Disarmament. (Affectionately known to its adherents as C.N.D.) This organisation prided itself upon its establishment-backing and its respectability, numbering in its ranks many prominent Fabians and academics who took good care to see that their own antics and activities were kept within the law. As time went on, however, the marches and the peaceful demonstrations outside the gates of the defence establishment were increasingly disrupted by a highly vociferous group of activists who succeeded in turning the whole affair into something between guerrilla warfare and a football riot. It was this particular faction which confronted the police and attempted a violent breakthrough into the research unit itself, — in course of which heads were broken and a number of the demonstrators arrested. They were reputed to belong to an organisation called the Committee of 100, which the police and the public at large assumed to be an adjunct of C.N.D.

After one particularly rowdy gathering, there was a correspondence in the Glasgow Herald which dealt sarcastically and abusively with the protesters, and suggested that their activities demanded a much wider interpretation of police powers. It also mentioned the fact that Mrs. Judith Hart, M.P. for South Lanark, had been prominently in attendance, and linked her name with the Committee of 100, who were widely assumed to be responsible for the violence.

Lawyers for Mrs. Hart promptly took up the matter with the Herald, denying that their client had ever had any association with the afore-mentioned Committee, and claiming that the inference was libellous. Grounds for the alleged libel were that the Committee of 100 was a *subversive organisation,* membership of which would have been incompatible with Mrs. Hart's position in public life, and imputed associations with which would damage her prospects in future elections.

The Herald's legal department were somewhat bemused by the whole proceedings. It should be explained that at this period in its long history the *Glasgow Herald* was an independent national newspaper revelling in the blessed autonomy which had been preserved for it by the late Lord Fraser of Allander. Its editorial staff were therefore blissfully unaware that there might be pitfalls ahead for those who loyally followed the line of God, Queen and Country. The offending correspondence was at least as sardonic as it had been abusive, and they had initially tended to treat the whole matter in a much lighter vein than either Mrs. Hart or her lawyers were disposed to do. They were in fact learning for the first time, — as was the author of the alleged libel, — that there were two distinct entities within the anti-nuclear protest movement at that time, — that one was subversive and the other reputedly non-subversive, and that the latter would go to great pains to distance itself from the former.

¶48. LEMMING DROVERS

In the analogy adopted throughout this volume, one might draw the distinction as between lemmings and lemming drovers. Mrs. Hart's case, — and after that Aldermaston incident of many years ago she got an out-of-court settlement to substantiate it, — was that she should be identified with the little furry lemming creatures, rather than with those who incited and urged them on. Likewise those who got themselves muddy bottoms by squatting in the mechanical shovels at Torness in the autumn of 1978 were protesting with their backsides, and did not otherwise disclose their ideologies or their convictions.

But locked in the legal files of the Glasgow Herald is an implied admission that at least one of the organisations campaigning to eliminate our nuclear deterrent during the nineteen-sixties was consciously subversive. Had it not been so, the M.P. for South Lanark would not have required to go to such lengths to disassociate herself from it. And whatever the legal niceties, it was made clear enough to the ordinary citizen by all Ban-the-Bomb agitators that their objective was to persuade, cajole, threaten or otherwise induce the British nation into a state of unilateral nuclear disarmament, — a state in which, as the rumbustious Nye Bevan once admitted, she would send her negotiators naked into the conference chamber.

So! lemmings or lemming drovers? Subversives conscious or sub-conscious? What does it matter? If these misguided people could not be persuaded to march, and squat, and sit in, the Soviets would either be obliged to abandon this particular line of subversion, or attempt to organise it themselves, — with results that might make their ambitions a bit more transparently obvious to the citizens of this befuddled land.

We might be somewhat more kindly disposed towards our conservationist lemming folk if we could be assured that there were indeed parallel campaigns and organisations behind the Iron Curtain, all the way from Moscow to Nijni Novgorod, and from the Black Sea to the outermost fringes of Siberia. Somehow this seems unlikely. After sixty years of authoritarian collectivism, purges and revolution, the Soviet lemming is virtually an extinct species, and the only logical end to anti-energy conservationist mania in our own country is to ensure that we ultimately fall behind in the race for resources.

Alternatively we could drop out of the race altogether. If we do, the next step is nuclear blackmail, — a plundering of our existing technology and resources by the then all-powerful Soviets, — our relegation to a quiet and miserable backwater, from which our citizens might be led off to forced labour in various parts of the Earth, virtually as twentieth century slaves.

"Stop everything! We've just
found a new endangered species.
"Isn't science wonderful?"

CHAPTER SEVEN
Anti-Nuclear Activities in Europe and U.S.A.

¶ 49.

At the moment of writing there seems every reason to suppose that the United Kingdom nuclear programme is adequate to carry us into the twenty-first century. This survey does not concern itself with design, location or environmental considerations in detail, merely with the ever-present danger that our scientists and technologists may be thwarted, through subversive ploys and delay tactics, from progressing and perfecting developments necessary to our future economic competitiveness and national security.

And for comparison, it may be useful to examine how the anti-nuclear protesters have been faring elsewhere. Sweden, a corporate state evolved on Fabian concepts, has no plans for developing nuclear energy at all. In Austria there was a closely contested referendum in November of 1978 upon whether the nation's first nuclear power station should be put into operation. The plant had been seven years in the building, at that time was almost complete, and had been designed to meet all the electricity requirements of the city of Vienna. By a margin of less than one per cent, the electorate voted *against*, and the Government had to cancel the project.

All right! it has been argued that the Soviets could take over Sweden with a telephone call, and since the dissolution of the Hapsburg Empire, Austria is never likely to compete in the big league again, so the fact that she has settled for remaining a non-nuclear backwater, whilst pleasing the conservationists, will scarcely have cataclysmic effects upon the balance of resources.

France, by contrast, has been getting on with it whilst others have been talking and arguing. The nation which, under de Gaulle, stepped huffily out of the North Atlantic Treaty, has since built up its own independently controlled nuclear deterrent, and continues in addition with a formidable programme for the industrial uses of nuclear energy, apparently without serious hindrance from its conservationist or environmental lobbies.

The French have been criticised for their stubborn reliance upon exclusively French know-how, and for their refusal to submit to any internationally imposed ban on nuclear testing. Unlike their Anglo-Saxon neighbours across the Channel, they never had any cause to delude themselves about "special relationships" with the United States, and as a result, created their own *force de frappe* which, small though it might be in comparison with the nuclear arsenals of the two super-powers, is yet a viable and immensely destructive weapon system that remains under the direct control of the French president.

¶ 50.
FRENCH INFLUENCE ON THE BALANCE OF TERROR

In this strange study of subversion and counter-subversion, we so often have to decide that what we once thought to be black is now white, — and conversely that what seemed white is either black, or differing shades of grey. That is exactly the situation with regard to the French, who so often have been presented to us as the mavericks of the Western Alliance, — the obstinate Gallic steers who said "non, non, non" to repeated requests for Britain to enter the Common Market, and whose antagonisms towards our transatlantic cousins are reciprocated in a love-hate relationship that has to be experienced to be appreciated.

The key to this black-is-white white-is-black conundrum is the foreign policy pursued over recent years by various United States governments, — a policy which from time to time has dismayed their friends, and generally delighted their enemies. Which of America's allies, for instance, could afford to trust the State Department after what happened to the Shah of Iran and President Samoza of Nicaragua? Others who had cause to treat it with the deepest suspicion were Dr. Savimbi of the Western-orientated U.N.I.T.A. movement in Southern Angola, and Bishop Muzorewa, first black prime minister of Zimbabwe-Rhodesia. Under Harold Wilson and Jim Callaghan, Britain was party to the diplomacy of the double-cross, and suffered herself from the old one-two whenever there was a conflict of interests.

So the Gallic cussedness which made the French pull out of NATO and set up their own deterrent, was a step which might have had far-reaching implications for the survival of Western Europe. Collectivists, from whatever side of the Iron Curtain, deplore independent action, since it can often be unpredictable, and jeopardise their plans. It may be that in the dangerous years of the mid-seventies, when several of the largest English-speaking democracies were controlled by weak indecisive governments heavily infiltrated by Marxist-Fabians with their ideological hearts in Moscow, the existence of an independent French nuclear deterrent, in the hands of a nationalist-minded autocrat, was one of the imponderables which dissuaded the Russians from exploiting their advantage.

AMERICAN CONSERVATIONISTS
¶51.   AND THE E.P.A.

In the United States, where they are reckoned to consume more than twice as much energy per head of population as any other industrialised nation, conservation is in the hands of a prestigious federal organisation called the Environmental Protection Agency, (E.P.A. for short). America needs conservation. As a young and bustling country a few decades ago, its farmers overcropped large areas of the central plains till they had created massive soil erosion, and pesticides and airborne fluorides emitted from chemical plants have crippled livestock and rendered parts of the surrounding countryside unfit for either animal or human occupation.

Undoubtedly some degree of environmental protection was badly needed, and a government agency sponsored and financed for that purpose should have commanded the support of all sane and thoughtful American citizens. The E.P.A. does not nowadays however enjoy such a reputation. Indeed in many of its zanier aspects it is being regarded with extreme suspicion.

An American journalist Alan Stang, writing in the John Birch magazine "American Opinion", points to one of the Agency's fads in the creation of an "endangered species" list. This phrase promptly brings to mind some of the efforts made in our own country to preserve the haunts of the eagle and the osprey, or the creation of the vast game parks in central Africa, where wild life is protected within its own environment, and allowed to survive and prosper outwith the range of man's rapacity or drive for technological progress. In an American context this might mean preserving the reindeer or the buffalo, sequestrating areas of parkland and mountain and high plateau where buck and racoon, leopard and jack rabbit, lizard and lynx, as well as reptile, fish and fowl, might continue their savage predatory existence, the hunter and the hunted, as nature had intended. With some two hundred and twenty million people, the U.S.A. is still by no means over-populated, and there would be no serious objection to the allocation of tracts of wilderness where man's furred and feathered friends, as well as many a scaly and shell-encrusted sub-species, might co-exist in harmony with himself.

But apparently there are powerful influences within the E.P.A. which do not see the regulations on "endangered species" purely as a means of preserving the environment. An order for the preservation of "the San Francisco garter snake and the red-legged frog" has been sought as a means to prevent a housing development in Oakland, California, and in Santa Cruz another project was allowed to go ahead on the condition that houses built on certain hillsides would be up on stilts, so that an *endangered species* called the long-toed salamander might safely pass underneath en route to its traditional watering place.

All right! these are the freaks and the zanies of the environmental protection business. They caused delays and heavy expense to some poor suckers who fancied their chances of a home in some secluded and previously unspoiled beauty spot. But there are now serious allegations that the "endangered species" regulations are being used, not only by zany environmentalists, but also by vested interests, for hampering and hamstringing the construction and development of projects vital to America's role as leader of the Free World. Alan Stang claims in fact that it is positively weird how often they have managed to find an *endangered species* living out its precarious existence within batting distance of some thermo-nuclear site, where work has inevitably to be abandoned while the developers and the conservationists battle it out together.

A BUREAUCRATIC SPECIES OF LEMMING

¶52.

This is undoubtedly an ingenious variation upon the relatively crude tactics of S.C.R.A.M. and *Friends of the Earth* and *Greenpeace*. It might set the whole anti-nuclear protest movement, aided by a summer school of Oxbridge insectologists, scrambling under rocks on the foreshore at Dunbar, to see if they could unearth some unique and hitherto unsuspected variety of bug, ant or tadpole, whose investigation and categorisation might hold up the construction and commissioning of the Torness nuclear station for an unspecified number of years.

Does that seem far-fetched from the British point of view? Happily it does. We have our troubles at the bureaucratic level, but not to the degree of refinement that has apparently been reached in the United States. Even our Judith Harts and Bertrand Russells, influential though they were from time to time within the political and academic establishments, were never able to orientate official thinking sufficiently in their own direction as to make other forms of dissent irrelevant. Resistance to the development of nuclear energy in this country has been relegated to the streets, to the site demos., to the fringe elements, to the sit-ins and sit-down protesters. It has apparently not manifested itself at a significant level within the bureaucracy, – and for that we must be truly thankful.

Bearing in mind that so many of the mistakes and pitfalls of American life get exported across here eventually, we should however be sufficiently interested in what is happening over there to ensure that we benefit from their experience. And it appears that in contrast to our own situation, resistance to development in the more sophisticated forms of energy is now thoroughly embedded within the Government itself. The lemming folk of Washington D.C. wear Yale and Harvard college ties, use conveyor belt techniques for the production of restrictions and inhibitions, and in their pursuit of regulation-mania, spawn upon large and ever-expanding federal budgets.

¶ 53.　　　　A SERIOUS ALLEGATION

In July of 1979, President Jimmy Carter, following a week-long seminar and discussion session in his retreat at Camp David, and in reaction to another price-hike in crude oil by the petroleum exporting countries of the Middle East, – announced a new energy policy for the United States which came down heavily on the side of conservation, but was lamentably and significantly weak in its proposals for increasing the amount of home-produced energy readily exploitable. It provided considerable resources for research into tides and solar panels, and though it did not specifically mention windmills, there was an implicit *something* in the tone of the speech that anyone who wanted to go back to the motive power of mediaeval Holland would be awarded a grant and the blessing of the Environmental Protection Agency. It appeared that Amory B. Lovins, the young man from the *Friends of the Earth* organisation who had made the headlines when he was published in the prestigious Rockefeller journal *Foreign Affairs,* was destined to become the new messiah and high priest of a "soft energy" America.

Support for such a policy was being strengthened by a whole army of governmental Jeremiahs who predicted the imminent exhaustion of global supplies of fossil fuels, and the

THE LEMMING FOLK

sombre picture of a cold and hungry planet which had depleted
its fuel structure and destroyed its own environment. Yet a U.S.
Congressman, Steven Symms, writing in September of 1978,
had claimed that on known reserves alone, and based on current
consumption rates, his country had an 84 years supply of crude
oil, 400 years of natural gas, 600 years of coal and 300 years of
oil shale, — not counting her ability to buy, produce and
process uranium for nuclear reactors. He suggested that the
election of President Jimmy Carter was a signal for the "zany
environmentalists" to crawl out of their ratholes, and that the
incessant and highly publicised drive for energy conservation
was in direct proportion to the taxes, regulatory inhibitions,
delays and frustrations that were being brought to bear upon
those who sought to explore and develop new energy sources.

This is a serious allegation. It infers that there are powerful
groups within the government bureaucracy who would revel in
the prospect of an America crestfallen and chastened, and at the
mercy of the Middle Eastern oil sheikhs. Congressman Symms
also points to big money pressure groups, research commissions
and "expert" loaded cultural, scientific and population control
programmes, many of which he identifies as communist fronts.
Apparently the best "front" that they have found thus far is the
American Conservation Lobby, which is now being showered
with funds, expertise and a measure of bureaucratic encouragement and immunity which enables it to engineer the most ex-
cruciating delays and procrastinations in the name of environmental purity.

In the last hundred years America has been powered
forwards and upwards because a vast majority of her citizens
believed implicitly in their country's organising and technical
ability, in the generous distribution of her natural resources, in
her capacity to plan and provide for the future, and in so doing
to provide a spin-off of wealth, trade and technology that
would benefit her allies and her neighbours. With the arrival of
Jimmy Carter in the White House there was constant pressure
from the top to change that outlook, and with it the traditional
American life-style. Why? Had the balance of energy sources and

reserves shifted so drastically in the previous few years?

MULTI-MILLIONAIRE WHO
¶54. ADVOCATES THE SIMPLE LIFE

Many Americans believed their government was simply not being honest with them in its conservation crusade, and that Jimmy Carter was as phony as his synthetic smile. They took it hard when Laurence Rockefeller, one of the four Rockefeller brothers, and multi-millionaire grandson of the original John D. Rockefeller, came forth as a leading American environmentalist, and preached to his countrymen that if only they would take up the simple life, demanding few amenities, they would be able to donate the remainder of their vast substance to the poorer peoples of the Third World.

All one can say at this stage is that if America took up the simple life as advocated by the plush-lined Rockefeller, adopted "soft energy" techniques as proposed by Amory B. Lovins and the zany conservationists, — became as a result a non-industrialised backwater, and allowed technological and industrial superiority to pass out of her hands, — it would be a poor prospect for the rest of us in the West, and there would be precious few amenities to share with the Third World, or anyone else.

Any more lemmings for drowning?

CHAPTER EIGHT

¶55. The Human Rights Lemming

This section deals with the habits and peregrinations of a species of blinkered lemming whose chief characteristic is a proclivity for seeing in one direction only. The human rights lemming is prominent in church committees and commissions, especially those with close affiliation to the W.C.C. It also proliferates in the trade unions, which were originally created to protect the rights and jobs of British workers, but which the ideological lemming has since adapted to spread the largesse abroad. The creature abounds on the professional side of politics, and can be seen at its best during certain foreign policy debates in the House of Commons.

Like many of the other causes espoused, infiltrated and finally taken over by Marxist-Fabianism, the issue of *man's inhumanity to man* can, in the immortal words of the poet Burns, *make countless thousands mourn.* No one disputes the ideal of removing discrimination, suffering and injustice from the face of the earth, — and where this ideal is pursued honestly, without fear or favour, its protagonists are everywhere worthy of the highest honour.

The trouble is that once an issue like human rights becomes politically motivated, it results in a vast increase of that type of suffering, privation and injustice which it was specifically designed to ameliorate, or for preference banish completely. The Soviets and their ideological sympathisers excuse this

81

LEMMUS MORALIS

A species of Human Rights Lemming
And exponent of selective indignation

somewhat repelling development by pointing out that their main purpose in promoting riot, social unrest and a never-ending succession of liberation movements throughout the western sphere of influence is to create a universal state of revolution wherein all will finally enjoy the benefits of collect-ivist egalitarianism, — and that, bearing in mind the reactionary attitudes of the Capitalist-Fascist-Imperialist governments who oppose them, it is quite inevitable there should be a vast increase of human suffering in the meantime.

¶ 56.   THE VIETNAM BOAT PEOPLE

In recent years the most utterly insensate, the most brutal and horrific violations of "human rights" have taken place in the former French colony of Indo-China. There, in the once gentle land of Cambodia, an extremist revolutionary group called the Khmer Rouge seized control with the aid of Communist arms, and proceeded to remove all possible traces of reaction or deviationism by imposing an immediate reign of terror. One of their early operations was to depopulate the city of Pnom Penh of its three million citizens, — forcibly, and without mercy or exception, — leaving the survivors to scratch for a living, sometimes without tools or foodstocks, in an inhospitable countryside.

Over the border, in the strip of coastal territory giving on to the Gulf of Tongking, an area which, after the departure of the French, came to be known as South Vietnam, there developed a situation which was to have wider consequences. In the second half of 1978 it became generally known that large numbers of Vietnamese were migrating from their homeland by the sea route, presumably the only escape route available to them in the circumstances. They were setting out in converted fishing boats, leaky sampans and all manner of small and medium coastal craft in differing degrees of seaworthiness. As the world gradually got to know more about them, it was realised that they were not landless peasants, nomads, criminals, racketeers or wastrels, but a cross-section of South Vietnam's commercial, professional and intellectual society, — people who had lived through the trauma of the eight-year Vietnamese War, but for previously undisclosed reasons, were unable to live through its aftermath.

So they had taken to the sea in large and larger numbers, often without adequate precautions for their victualling, medical care and general safety *en voyage*, and totally without advance provision for their reception as refugees on some distant and possibly unsympathetic shore. They became known as the Vietnam "boat people", and though many of them perished from disease or malnutrituion, or when their frail and unsuitable craft foundered in stormy seas, in virtually unlimited numbers they simply kept on coming, — in many cases pledging all their worldly assets to pay for their passages to a totally unknown future.

The new Communist government of South Vietnam knew that they were going. If there was no attempt to assist them, neither was there any attempt to hinder, — and the fact that passages had to be paid in gold brought in from abroad, indicated that the whole migratory movement had developed into a licensed trade in human lives, out of which the regime itself intended to extract the maximum benefit.

¶57.   YANKS GO HOME

Whatever way one looks at it, this is one of the most traumatic tales of our own, or indeed any century. Lucid, well-balanced, formerly successful commercial and professional people, sometimes burdened with aged parents and young families, selling up the assets acquired in half-a-lifetime of patient endeavour, — all to buy passages in some ancient freighter or overcrowded coastal steamer, whose captain had been commissioned to drop them virtually anywhere, so long as it was outside of Communist Vietnam! Educated people, of responsible years, and in sound mind, — presumably knowing the fate of many who had gone before, — yet asked to choose between a watery grave and life under communism, opting invariably for the hazards and the uncertainties of that boat journey to nowhere!

Was this not a devastating indictment of the system that had been imposed upon South Vietnam as a result of the anti-war protest movement which swept America in the late nineteen-sixties, and the success of which ensured that this far-off Asiatic country would have communism, whether it wanted it or not? For the Yanks had not pulled out because they were defeated militarily. All the time they had possessed the striking power, the strategic panache and the economic and technological back up to starve and harass Ho Chi Minh's thinly spread guerrilla warriors out of existence, — it would be a truly traumatic prospect for eventual Western survival if things had ever been otherwise. But always it seemed that there was a political decision to overrule the instincts of the soldiers in the field; lateral restrictions placed upon the bombing of the Vietcong supply trails; failure to follow up the initiative gained by the mining of Haiphong Harbour; a strange lack of dedication to the objective of total victory.

It had happened to Douglas MacArthur some fifteen years earlier. Soldiers involved in a war run by politicians are exposed to both physical and psychological risks more inhibiting than anything they might encounter on the field of battle. There was no one of MacArthur's stature in Saigon who might justifiably put his career on the line by confronting the political leadership with its contradictions and vacillations. Vietnam became the no-win war, — with a predictable drop-off in military morale and enthusiasm. The protests on the university campuses became more strident and more fanatical. Nightly the television networks penetrated American living rooms with their skilfully documented tales of war weariness and disillusionment. A Hollywood film star got herself notoriety by openly going over to the Vietcong. Journalists and editors of the Fabian-orientated national newspapers daily flirted with treason by offering aid and comfort to the enemy. A whole society seemed about to tear itself apart upon the dilemma of what to do about containing communism in a one-time fairyland of gentle folk and ancient Buddhist culture. Faced by this barrage of defection and defamation, in 1972 President Richard Nixon began the process of de-escalation and withdrawal. Communist conquest of South Vietnam took place almost immediately after the Yanks had taken the advice of their own protesters, and had made their way home.

¶58.   PROFIT FROM HUMAN MISERY

So the trauma and tragedies of the Vietnam boat people had been a direct consequence of the countless riots and demonstrations on university campuses all the way from Harvard to Berkeley, California. This was one of the most significant victories of the Third World War, and it had been won, — not by hardened revolutionaries, — but by thousands of footloose young people bored and disenamoured with their studies, ready to take up any cause which gave them a chance to wave banners, make a noise and join in communal activity. These were the human rights lemmings of the nineteen-sixties, — who by their contribution to the Protest Movement, would help to precipitate the worst human rights atrocity of the late twentieth century.

The strident and hysterical demand for peace had brought no peace, — only a vast proliferation of human misery, — not directly affecting those young students at Harvard and Berkeley, many of whom came from good-class American homes, and who would perhaps be comfortably settled in their chosen professions before the boat people set out on their hazardous journeys. So how is the West to be warned of the evils of communism if it will not harken to the miseries and privations of those who have experienced it at first hand?

In this strange topsy-turvy world of *nuspeak*, double think and an ideological motivation for countless forms of otherwise innocent human activity, it is not enough to feel with the heart. It is also necessary to think with the head. In *realpolitik* the collectivist adversary is doing this all the time, — and in the affair of the Vietnam boat people the long-term objective was enunciated in terms of unmistakeable clarity by Lee Kuan Yew, the Prime Minister of Singapore, when he visited London in June of 1979.

He pointed out that a large proportion of the migratory

"boat people" were ethnic Chinese whom, after its contretemps with Peking, the Vietnamese Government would obviously find expendable. There were several million members of this racial minority who could be persuaded or harassed into leaving Vietnam as refugees, and the pressures engendered by an oncoming horde of deprived and suffering humanity could set up severe strains within the economies of neighbouring countries who would feel constrained to provide for them. This in turn could serve the interests and further the ambitions of the Hanoi government, – for not only would it embarrass and weaken the administrations of the host countries by setting them almost insurmountable problems of integration and re-settlement, but there would also be opportunity to infiltrate among the migrants any number of *agents provocateurs* who would be well placed to assist in the future "liberation" of all South-East Asia.

So said Lee Kuan Yew, – and from his own ethnic back-ground and geographical location, he is a man who ought to know. Not only do we have a gross breach of human rights, – we also have it on sound authority that this breach of human rights is being exploited to further the aims of psychopolitical warfare. Another phase in fact of this Third World War, whose battles still go largely unreported!

Racial discrimination! Inhuman methods of deportation! A government profiting directly from the trade in human misery! No lack of pretext and opportunity here for our human rights crusaders to raise their banners, plan their boycotts and stage their demonstrations! So how have they responded to this unprecedented situation?

Mostly with a heavy deliberating silence! Not that some of them would not be active in other directions! Consolidating their threats and their reprisals against counter-revolutionary government in Chile for instance! Or joining in the everlasting barrage of abuse, condemnation, innuendo and disinformatory propaganda against *apartheid* in South Africa! Doesn't the human rights lemming sicken you with his hypocrisy?

THE ANTI-APARTHEID LEMMING

CHAPTER NINE

¶59. The Anti-Apartheid Lemming

One significant difference between South Vietnam, (no acknowledged violation of human rights), and South Africa (human rights reputedly being violated all the time), is that whereas undetermined numbers of people are struggling to escape from the former, the problem with the latter is how to stop more and more would-be immigrants from getting in. So it would appear that the prevailing international standards on human rights do not necessarily indicate the desirable spots in which to live. Africans flocking to get inside the borders of white-controlled South Africa must be motivated by other considerations than those propagated by the anti-apartheid movement in the U.K. Higher living standards for instance, better wages, superior housing perhaps, — greater security for themselves and their families, — than they had enjoyed in the territories whence they came!

So why is it that South Africa has become the *cause célèbre* for anti-discrimination leagues, human rights and civil liberties associations the world over? How can you get unanimous condemnations of *apartheid* in women's rurals, trade union branch meetings, university debating societies, church assemblies, business men's conventions and gay rights groups, — with the same facility that one would employ to get a motion in favour of free beer at a brewers' centenary? Why do the most vehement denunciations come from those with least practical experience of the problem, — ethnically pure Swedish Socialists who know nothing about multi-racialism until they go abroad on package tours; left-wing editorials which champion the closed shop in industrial matters, but are apparently opposed to any other form of selectivity; wet little get-togethers of the N.U.S., financed by taxpayer contributions, eagerly extending associate membership to the new generation of Che Guevaras, and lavishly quoted down to the least responsible of its adolescent pronouncements by a sensation-seeking daily press purportedly searching for the voice of youth?

Corrupt and incompetent politicians, power-lusting union bosses, sadistic black dictators, administrative fiddlers, mafia gangsters, and all manner of crooks, conspirators, con. men and opinion moulders who feed upon human prejudice and credulity, must be heartily grateful for the perennial *apartheid* issue, to the extent that it distracts attention from their own illegal aims and felonies. But the houh-ha is all orchestrated and manipulated, and people of vision have recognised this long ago.

There are evils in South African society, as indeed there are in most others. She has slums and ghettos, and wide areas where discrimination is the rule rather than the exception. She has a police service which still uses strong arm methods, and which may tend to come down harder if the suspect happens to be black. Her moods and her policies are continually changing, not drastically, but bit by bit, as positive ideas emerge from beneath or from outside.

The changes which are desirable will come anyway, as South Africans realise that they have to live with each other, regardless of creed or colour. The changes which are planned under pressure from external boycotts, or from internal subversion financed and monitored by the clandestine forces of world revolution, could only come after the Afrikaaners had been driven into the sea, and through total destruction of a social and economic base whose preservation is vital to the living standards of all Southern Africa.

Any starry-eyed anti-apartheid crusader want to argue with the practical wisdom of that hypothesis? Any human rights devotees sincerely feel that the absolute priority in their march towards social justice is to throw fifteen million people into a state of anarchy from which many will not escape with their lives?

SOVIET STRATEGY IN
¶60.   SOUTHERN AFRICA

Those who make their judgments in *realpolitik*, — rather than the guff and gobble-de-gook of the mass communications industry, — have long realised that South Africa's insistence on an *apartheid* solution to her racial problems is by no means an adequate explanation for the concerted economic and political offensive that has been mounted against her from the four corners of the earth. In so far as the attack is ideological in character, — subversive and revolutionary, — it is simple enough to associate it with International Communism's grand design of encircling the Western powers before moving in for the kill.

The strategic significance of the Cape of Good Hope has been quoted more than often as an obvious pretext for the Soviet eagerness to advance their sphere of influence right down to the tip of Southern Africa, — and the manner in which that is likeliest to come about, via unstable black governments, arti-ficially stimulated tribal war, popular disillusion and economic cataclysm, — is ideal for their purposes. With their own puppets duly installed as presidents and war ministers, there would be no reluctance to set up the necessary alliances, — and once Soviet submarines started operating out of the naval base at Simonstown, the Western World would effectively be split in two.

Such is how anti-communist strategists have seen it for many years, — and it is a threat that cannot be dismissed lightly. For its success it needs the dedicated co-operation of lots and lots of lemming folk, — human rights, anti-apartheid, and all manner of idealists and starry-eyed splinter groups who would be the last to realise how they were being conned. Even so, judging by previous Soviet successes in psychopolitical warfare, who is to say that, allied to some sabre-rattling and terrorism at appropriate moments, the policy would not succeed?

91

In more recent years, however, there has been a dramatic reappraisal of the scope and the alignments of the forces bent on destroying the Boer Republic south of the Limpopo. Soviet involvement is there in plenty, – in the training and arming of terrorists, and the planting of subversives to stir up the indigenous population. But the massive scope of the propaganda assault seemed more than the Russians themselves could sustain, with their extended supply lines and limited base facilities in Lusaka. It seemed that there had to be someone else, someone who did not lack for money, or the right of entrée to the most sensitive spots of psychological pressure.

AMERICAN DOLLARS THAT
¶61.   FINANCE REVOLUTION

Observers had known for some time that several of the very wealthy American tax-exempt foundations, having declared their opposition to *apartheid*, were an easy touch for any "freedom" or "liberation" groups who professed to be active in the same cause. There were also prominent Fabian-inspired organisations such as the League for Industrial Democracy and Americans for Democratic Action, the latter of which, perfecting the subtle psychopolitical tactics of *anti*-anti-communism, had smeared and effectively destroyed Senator McCarthy and his Committee of un-American Activities.

Americans had founded and funded a legal body somewhat clumsily entitled *Lawyers' Committee for Civil Rights under the Law,* and this was being used as both an advisory and a financing service for subversives brought before the South African courts for treason or conspiracy. In addition, active opposition to *apartheid* was being co-ordinated through a vast network of human rights associations, civil liberties unions, church groups, women's clubs, and any other facet of social, industrial or religious life which could be expected to touch the palpitating liberal conscience of the U.S.A.

Was this, then, a full and adequate explanation of the increasingly evident and embarrassing fact that the assault on South Africa was being bankrolled, – not by the Russian rouble or the Chinese yuan, – but by good old American dollars for which credit had been created in Washington or New York? Could it be that this surreptitious drive to destroy a major United States trading partner was getting its cash and its moral resolution from the dime, dollar and ten-spot contributions of U.S. private citizens and corporate bodies to whom the racist implications of *apartheid* were an affront and an evil more to be confronted and eliminated than any other evil on the face of the earth?

Was the American lemming going to prove himself much bigger and much more self-destructive than his British counterpart? Or being a citizen of the world's largest democracy, did he not regard himself as a lemming at all? Did he assume that America was so secure in her continental hegemony that she could gratuitously discard all her erstwhile friends and allies, whilst remaining herself invulnerable?

¶ 62.
THE C.I.A. AND THE U.S. CAVALRY

Certain obscure and not too well publicised factors made this explanation implausible. Firstly those tax-exempt American foundations which had been so generous in funding Southern African subversive, terrorist and black power movements, – it had been pointed out that they would lose their tax-exempt status if they were found to be pursuing policies contrary to the interest of the U.S. Government. One such organisation, the American Friends Service Committee, is quoted by Aida Parker (Secret U.S. War against South Africa) as having been investigated as far back as 1954 by the U.S. House Special Committee on its communist-front affiliations. It had then received more than a million dollars from the Ford Foundation, and there was no indication that either the latter or the Friends Committee had incurred governmental disapproval as a result.

Then there was the intriguing and mystifying role played in all this by the C.I.A. This highly classified anti-espionage outfit, formed as an intelligence wing of the U.S. security forces, had set up many a contradictory and self-defeating ploy in recent years and was reckoned to be largely responsible for the fact that the U.S. cavalry, which for almost half-a-century had been riding to the rescue in the nick of time, had now started arriving late and in the wrong places, — and when it did arrive, was finding itself both outgunned and out-manoeuvred by the local Injuns.

A sad reflection upon the myopic and inadequate efforts of a once proud and self-confident Uncle Sam! And it was all happening because the C.I.A., which should have been his eyes and ears, had either developed double vision, or was practising the good old-fashioned double-cross. In this latter connection, many patriotic Americans, disgusted by their Intelligence Agency's utter incompetence in protecting their country's interests, came to the conclusion that the C.I.A. was no longer a single organisation, that it had somehow acquired a subversive wing, and that this latter was conspiring to thwart and frustrate the responsible activities of its legitimate alter ego.

But what? when? where? how? Would there never be an end to this conspiratorial tangle? Who were the goodies, who were the baddies? And just what was the real objective of this high-pressure, multi-million dollar campaign, masterminded by a maverick offshoot of the C.I.A., and financed by Wall Street's tax-exempt foundations, for the economic and political destruction of South Africa?

CHAPTER TEN

¶ 63. **The Capitalist Lemming**

At this stage, whilst the mind is still boggling at the prospect of an official department of the U.S. Government actively working to destroy the economy of a major trading partner, it is necessary to bring wriggling out of the nest a surprising little chap, complete with city bowler, pin-striped suit and rolled umbrella. The capitalist lemming!

But who ever heard of such a phenomenon? Everyone who has ventured thus far in the study of lemming folk has convinced himself that this type of suicidal aberration is exclusively for the lower orders. When the Anti-Nazi League and the S.W.P. go into the streets in search of recruits, it's the coloured immigrant, the unemployed, the maladjusted and the under-privileged whom they expect to give them a hearing. They don't go to the city chaps in the bars and coffee houses round the Stock Exchange, and they don't waste much time in the suburban stockbroker belt either.

Psychopolitics is all about a fiendishly clever and surreptitious method of bringing about class revolution without the mass of the people being aware of what is happening. And since revolution is paramountly concerned with the destruction of capitalism, surely the last group the revolutionaries would expect to assist them would be the capitalists themselves.

Well maybe so! But remember that remark of Father Lenin's that when they came to hang the last capitalist, it would

95

THE CAPITALIST LEMMING

So closely involved with his world of banking, investment and finance, that he might fail to see the fallacies . . . ?

be with his own rope, and he would pay the expenses of his own hanging.

MONEY AND BRAINS
¶64.   AMONG THE SUBVERSIVES

Ha! ha! quite funny! more than a grain of truth in it too! Obviously a reference to the greed of some of those commercial chaps who profess not to give a damn about politics or principles, and who will trade with anyone, on any set of conditions, so long as they make a profit.

Then of course there's the type who, after a long spell of Socialist government, gets so hooked on grants and subsidies that the thought of a free economy gives him a sudden attack of nausea. That happened to a section of Britain's senior and middle management when Jim Callaghan gave way to Margaret Thatcher in May of 1979.

But look here! these fellows were still a long way from conniving at subversion, and becoming unwitting stooges in a plot to harm the state. They voted Conservative, didn't they? In spite of their unconscious leanings towards state corporatism, they're still solid for God, Queen and Country. What's more! you're not talking about a bunch of morons. Some of the sharpest investment and market analysts in the business! Can read a balance sheet with a facility with which the rest of us sip tea. Also, using their wits and their expertise of a lifetime, they've made a bit between them. You're not going to persuade *that* particular section of the population to join in some collectivist revolution. Well, are you?

Two points need to be made at this stage; firstly, that in the opinion of many students of *revolution*, these social cataclysms are rarely engineered by the masses whom they are professedly intended to benefit, — that they take both money and brains, which are more often found at the top than in the lower stratas of society; secondly, that in psychological warfare, — which this is all about, — it is fatal to become rooted in fixed loyalties of class or custom or cherished belief. Show him an idol of your adoration, and in due course of time the psychopolitical subversive will make it crumble before your eyes. Exhibit a weakness of sentiment or of conceit, and he will exploit that weakness till he has enlisted it for his own malign purposes.

Be on your guard from as sturdy a watchtower as you can assemble, restlessly scan three sides of the horizon, — and even then there is no guarantee that he will not strangle you from behind. In psychopolitics one of the most helpful, most enduring qualities is humility, a readiness to change stance and direction, to admit error and adapt to changing circumstances. What you don't ever do is to change your moral precepts, discard your religion or your principles. If you once do that, they've got you in the collectivist bag, and you wake up some day to find you're working for the opposition.

¶65.
FABIANS AND THE CLASSLESS SOCIETY

The Gradualist Revolution of the British Fabians, (studied at some length in "The Mind Benders"), was very much an upper class conception. The early Fabians thought of themselves as an élite, both in terms of breeding and mental stature, and in course of time they drew adherents from many of England's moneyed and aristocratic families. Theirs was to be the Revolution which would encompass, circumvent, subvert and manipulate all other revolutions, and it is upon the groundwork so carefully laid by the Fabians that our modern generation of collectivist conspirators have built the monster which we fear today.

Despite their middle and upper class backgrounds, and their innate dispositions towards élitism, the Fabians soon got down into the market place and the common debating houses, and started peddling the theories which would give them instant appeal with the masses. In the Merry England of the late nineteenth century their most dramatic advances were made when they attacked barriers which had been erected solely on the grounds of class. Classless society! that is a slogan and an ideal which has lasted them for the whole of this century. People don't like to think of themselves as inferior, — no matter how humble their station in life, or how indifferent their education, ability or qualifications. Religion had been strong among the poor and the under-privileged when it was the only arm of the Establishment which insisted that all human beings were equal before God. Now the masses were to find fascination and appeal in a new philosophy which preached equal rights for all citizens in a planned socialist society.

A PRIVILEGED ELITE AMONGST THE WORKERS

¶66.

Fabianism has been irresistibly successful in the hundred years of its existence because it has continued to preach theories about equality. It has somehow conveyed the impression that by a bit of manipulation and a considerable application of "social engineering", the good life, the leisurely expansive life, could be brought within the reach of all. When it spoke about *privilege,* the rarities and the advantages of *privilege*, and insisted that under "gradual change" all *privilege* must be abolished, it left the unspoken thought that those rarities and advantages would somehow be spread manifestly around, – not that they would totally disappear, or simply be assumed by a new type of privileged class, – the Fabians themselves.

For they had always intended to remain as an élite, – a highly selective intellectual élite gleaned from the top scholars, the top thinkers, the top academics of each generation. They it was who would mastermind the changes, the gradual but irreversible changes that would bring about the Revolution. The image that they conveyed was both élitist and populist, – élitist for the concentration of scholarship and brain power, – but at the same time populist because the alleged purpose of their (selfless) urge to change society was to change it in such a way that the riches of the Earth would be spread broadly and uniformly across the whole human race.

So for all their snobbery and élitism, and the undoubtedly privileged backgrounds from which many of them had descended, they could afford to be openly and unashamedly pro-working class, pro-proletariat, since their professed function in society was to implement a mild-mannered socialist-type revolution which would progressively free the working classes, the wage or salary-earning multitudes, from the shackles placed upon them by grasping, money-grubbing capitalism.

In this way their influence upon the working class politics of the country was clearly established. Fabians in fact would boast that it was their sure and stable foundation among the workers that had enabled them to progress forwards and ever upwards to the very pinnacles of power. Fabians from privileged backgrounds have held safe Labour seats in some of the most deprived areas of England's decaying cities. You can always find a Fabian lordship to plead a populist cause in the ermine-quilted House of Lords. Fabians lead the debates on municipalisation of housing and desegregation of schools, — whilst their own children go to the most selective schools in the land, — and it was they who tied the Labour Movement to nationalisation of production, distribution and exchange. All good revolutionary causes! All calculated to invite the enthusiastic support of the underprivileged, the unpropertied, the jobless, the helpless, the hopeless, the drop-out, — throughout the length and breadth of the land! That is what the Fabians are *for*. *For* the workers! *For* the unprivileged! *For* the losers, the failures and the unfortunates!

¶67.   ENTER THE CAPITALIST-MONOPOLIST

Let us now discover what the Fabians are supposed to be *against*, — for it was once remarked by a man who had complete confidence in the common sense of ordinary people, that you could not rally the honest-to-goodness fervour of the working community by talking to them in abstracts. You had to show them the enemy.

It therefore stands to reason that the Fabians have not had their fantastic success over the last century without presenting their supporters with a credible and visible enemy. Now who or what would that enemy be? Would it not be identified as *capitalism*, — money-grubbing reactionary capitalism, supra-national, cartelist power-hungry capitalism based upon faceless banking consortiums with their headquarters in Paris or Strasbourg or New York? Agreed?

In the transcript of the appeal launched by Bishop Donal Lamont of Umtali before the Rhodesian Supreme Court in March of 1977, it was mentioned in evidence that when a group of Z.A.Ñ.U. guerrillas (or freedom fighters) invested a Roman Catholic mission in south-eastern Rhodesia, they lined up the nuns and friars and subjected them to a harangue about the evils and iniquities of the capitalist-internationalist bankers in New York. Is it not therefore reasonable to assume that other forces of "freedom fighters", choking from the dusty sands of the Sahara, cutting their way through the impenetrable jungles of Brazil, roaming the pampas of Argentina, scaling the mountains of Chile or wading the monsoon swamps of South-East Asia, have been indoctrinated with chapter and verse on the iniquities of the self-same capitalist-monopolist enemy?

So the socialist pamphleteer in the streets of London or Birmingham, the freedom fighter in the bush or jungle, the shop steward on the factory floor of the supranational complex in Frankfurt or Glasgow, Bilbao or Barcelona, have all come to recognise that one common enemy, the faceless monolith of the Capitalist-Reactionary Money Power. That is what the Fabians are *against*. That is likewise what the working classes of all nations are apparently *against*, and the guerrillas in African and South American jungles are *against*.

THE FABIANS GET THEIR
¶68.   FINANCIAL MUSCLE

This being established, another argument surely follows, — that whoever dares to raise his voice in criticism of Fabianism or Worker Power or Revolution, — or any of the other joyful slogans in the glorious surge towards an emancipation of all humanity, must surely be part of the capitalist-reactionary system itself. They have a name for them in good class Marxist revolutionary circles. They call them lackeys, or lickspittles of their capitalist masters.

101

So the battle lines are clearly drawn. On my left the Fabians, — champions of the underdog and the under-privileged! On my right the Capitalists, the industrial monopolists and the international bankers, the cartelists, the manipulators of the money and commodity markets.

Is that it? Have we got it broadly in perspective? If we have, the first point which emerges is that it must at one time have been a very unequal battle, — the workers and their champions the Fabians, with literally all the money in the world against them. So how have they managed, down through the years, to wage such a successful war against this massive financial monolith?

In "The Mind Benders" it was coyly hinted that, at least in the latter period of their century-old struggle, the Fabians and their allies have not been without resources, — over and above the fact that they got their first send off with the help of some good old English aristocratic fortunes. Latterly the money came through wielding the levers of political and administrative power, — a power freely granted to them through the ballot box, as a result of their strong base within the working class movement.

So the changing image is of the exponents of Gradual Revolution slowly wresting the strongholds of financial and monopolistic power away from the banker and the cartelist, and doing it by the orthodox, traditional socialist method of nationalisation, municipalisation and sometimes downright appropriation, — all methods which in varying circumstances are thoroughly approved by their adherents, since no matter how immoral and unethical the *means*, it is all for an eminently desirable *end*, — the final and total emancipation of the working classes.

There we have at least one credible explanation for the fact that nowadays the Fabians seem to have access to unlimited supplies of money, — that they have won it forthrightly and honestly through achieving fiscal and political power over governments and taxation, — desirable social types of taxation which re-distribute wealth and incomes. In that respect they have done it without really compromising in their battle with the capitalist enemy.

Suppose at this stage we were to suggest, however, that there *had* been such a compromise, — that for many years now the Fabians have not been waging the class struggle from their own side of the battle lines, — aided only by the widow's mite, the labourer's shilling and the odd legacy from a conscience-stricken aristocrat. Suppose we were to argue that on recent evidence those smooth urbane élitists *have betrayed their working class allies* by going over to the enemy, and were continuing the drive towards global revolution from within the Capitalist-Monopolist power structure itself. Suppose we argued this! Depending upon your pre-conceived attitudes and your social background, how would you receive it? Scornfully? With frank disbelief? With suspicions of a red herring thrown in by the desperate reactionaries of property and privilege?

¶69.
RICHES BEYOND THE DREAMS OF AVARICE

What we have to set down now is not based upon theory or surmise, — upon what the author himself believes to be a logical extension of the Fabian Gradual Revolution in its ultimate drive towards global monopoly power. In other words, it is less a matter of dreaming up facts to suit the hypothesis than it is an effort to achieve some understanding of the realities of power politics in our own day. Neither does the author claim any credit for the researches or the conclusions, the sources of which will be mentioned as we progress.

The next exercise for all of us is to start thinking about wealth, — not the sudden influx of affluence which might come to the ordinary mortal after winning the treble chance, or from a rich uncle suddenly dying off in Australia, — but immoral, arrogant, overweening super-wealth so enormous that the average person could not hope to spend it all, even if he worked at it night and day for half a lifetime, — wealth such as lies in bank vaults, or in the balance sheets of large corporations. What sort of individuals do we find with such enormous wealth nowadays?

Queen Juliana of the Netherlands, with her holdings in Royal Dutch Shell? King Ibn Saud of Saudi Arabia? The Gettys? The Fords? The — Rockefellers?

We stop with the last named. All the others are in the millionaire class, and unlikely ever to touch their bottom dollars. But the Rockefellers are in a class by themselves. Descended from John D. Rockefeller Senr., who founded Standard Oil Company of New Jersey, the Rockefeller family has proved to be the big fish which ultimately swallows all the others. Its total wealth and assets may never be revealed, and even a rough assessment would defeat the ordinary investigator, since they or their representatives employ a crosslinking control of an undisclosed number of companies. In addition to *Exxon*, probably the largest oil company in the world, they also own a considerable slice of the Chase Manhattan Bank, which Gary Allen, author of "The Rockefeller File", has described as being "virtually a sovereign state".

When Nelson Rockefeller, grandson of the great John D., was appointed Vice President of the U.S.A. by Gerald T. Ford, the first fumbling effort to disclose his personal assets to the appropriate Senate sub-committee came up with some thirty-three million dollars. Some searching questions by suspicious legislators soon detected errors and omissions in this assessment, however, and a later submission placed the total at nearer *two hundred* million dollars, upon which basis Allen reckoned that the Vice President's financial experts had initially missed their target by an error of some six hundred per cent. When Nelson Rockefeller died of a sudden heart attack in the early months of 1979, his estate would already have been publicly stated at over *three hundred million* dollars.

THE WORLD'S MOST INFLUENTIAL
¶70. FAMILY

Of the three other Rockefeller brothers who had controlled the family empire since the Second World War, John D. the Third, who died in a car accident in 1977, was chairman of the Rockefeller Foundation, and a leading protagonist of world population control; Laurence busied himself with various liberal causes; and David, described by some people as the most powerful man in the world, had risen to become chairman of the Chase Manhattan Bank, where, to quote Allen again, he commanded more financial muscle than the Treasury of many a nation state. Add to this total the accredited control of publishing houses, newspaper chains, billions of dollars tucked away in undeclared assets at home and abroad, and the Rockefellers could scarcely shrink from the title of the world's most influential family.

O.k. So we've proved the point that the Rockefellers are rich, — super-super rich. But this is a chapter about capitalists, — and capitalists don't turn against fellow capitalists just because they happen to be in a much bigger league than themselves.

But one thing we *have* done is to name the target for all those Marxists, Trotskyists, Maoists, subversives and freedom fighters throughout the world who are busy stirring up causes and pretexts for social revolution. When the comrades get their political lectures in the jungles of South America, or in base camps on the fringes of Rhodesia and South Africa, the hate symbol which is held up to sustain their flagging efforts is that of the millionaire bankers, the Kennedys and the Rockefellers, who have their wicked and opulent headquarters in far off New York.

Likewise, when our own home-based revolutionaries are plodding their way through a hard stint of meetings and demonstrations, nothing eases their aching feet better than a personal pep session against the same immoral concentration of big wealth and power.

¶71. ROCKEFELLERS IN LEFT-WING ACTIVITIES

So we have identified even more clearly what the Fabians and the Marxists are commonly reckoned to be *against*. We have also established *who* they are against. The name is Rockefeller, symbol of obscene wealth, monopoly capital and reactionary privilege throughout the world.

But how have the four Rockefeller brothers themselves borne up under the burden of becoming ritualistic hate symbols for several generations of social reformers, egalitarian philosophers, shop floor agitators, Hyde Park Corner anarchists and class revolutionaries all the way from Seattle to Key West, from Glasgow's Red Clydeside southwards across the Equator to the Socialist black states of Southern Africa? Has it made them more confirmed in their capitalist principles than ever? Or like the conscience-stricken aristocrats of Tsarist Russia, have they developed a complex about their monopoly power, and endeavoured to spread their wealth outwards and downwards for the benefit of humanity in general?

Well John D. the Third, in his days at the centre of the campaign for World Population Control, managed to work amicably in harness with some unsavoury characters who were certainly no friends of Capitalist America. And Nelson, the one who went into politics, was always to be found in the Liberal, or left-leaning side of the Republican Party. In fact this was reckoned by some commentators to be his personal tragedy, that whilst he had chosen to be associated with the traditional party of Big Business, he had never really been trusted there, and might have achieved more of his ambitions had he crossed the floor and joined the Democrats, with whom ideologically he seemed to have more in common.

What's this? A left-leaning multi-millionaire? Liberal perhaps! But not Socialist surely — especially after we've been told that there are really very few Socialists in the United States! Could it be that among them there was a Rockefeller?

¶72.
FABIAN TEACHING FOR THE SONS OF CAPITALIST AMERICA

Let us look backwards into the early educational training of those Rockefeller brothers who were growing up in a changing world about the time of the First World War. Rose Martin reports, somewhat significantly, in "Fabian Freeway", that Nelson and David went to the Lincoln School of Columbia University, and that there they were exposed to the "progressive" educational methods of John Dewey, renowned as one of the Founding Fathers of Fabian Socialism in the United States. Stripped of Fabian guff, — that delicate legerdemain in word play which is intended to obfuscate the true meaning and direction of revolutionary tactics, — Dewey's "progressive" education, so cleverly exploited also by the Webbs and their associates in the United Kingdom, was simply a device for permeating the corrosive doctrines of Marxist-collectivism into some of the wealthiest American households.

It used to be argued for the Roman Catholic Church that if you gave them a child in its formative years, you could have it back for the rest of its life, and still not eradicate the effects of that early training. Well David and Nelson, fledgeling heirs to the vast and growing Rockefeller empire, apparently got Fabianism at an age when they were scarcely old enough to know what life was all about, and it remained to be seen how enduring, how limpet-like were the ideas that had been fastened on to them by the socialist teachings of John Dewey.

It is quite impossible for us to look closely into the complex minds of two powerful and important men, one of whom is now dead. Perhaps it is also unfair at this stage to judge the force and the relevance of the collectivist doctrine when those two super-rich young Americans first imbibed it in the nineteen twenties. We must remember that there was a day, — not long gone, — when Marxist-Fabian political theory, along with its deadly twin Keynesian economics, were reckoned to be the graven images at whose shrine the whole of humanity would come to worship for the indefinite future.

David and Nelson, having at their disposal the most expensive, if not the best advice that money could buy, may have decided that in face of this creeping collectivist revolution, the clever way to protect the family fortunes was to ride along with it. The judgments should not therefore be made too hastily, but only in the light of how the brothers decided to rationalise their problem.

These facts are now history, and are becoming progressively available to a wider public. Nelson joined the Liberal wing of

the Republican Party, where he no doubt hoped that a slavish
adherence to Fabian principles, plus a lavish infusion of Rockefeller dollars, would eventually carry him into the White House.
He made this target in the final years of his life, but only after
Watergate, and as assistant to Gerald T. Ford, whom the Establishment later dumped in favour of Jimmy Carter.

¶73.
ROCKEFELLER AND THE
BILDERBERG CONFERENCES

David, who strikes one at this distance as being the wiliest
and most resourceful of the Rockefeller brothers, steered well
clear of democratic processes, and worked himself into positions
of immense power from which he was unlikely to be dislodged
by popular approbium. As has been noted, it was he who took
control of the Chase Manhattan, with its umpteen hundred outlets in many countries, and powers of dispensation and patronage
greater than that of a nation state. He also became in due course
chairman of the Council on Foreign Relations, which, — as every
schoolboy should now be getting to know, — is an unelected
advisory body on foreign affairs set up by the Fabian Colonel
House, and reckoned under David Rockefeller's generalship to
have grown into a veritable "invisible government" of the United
States.

In 1950 or thereabouts, the C.F.R. started an ambitious
experiment in top secret internationalist collaboration when it
planned to involve in its own schemes a highly selective gathering
of Western Europe's leading bankers, financiers, scientists and
politicians. Only men — and the odd woman — with definite
power potential in their own countries, were considered worthy
of an invite. The first conference took place at the Bilderberg
Hotel in Holland in 1952, and thenceforth there were annual
meetings, sometimes in Europe, sometimes on the American
continent, until 1975, by which time the group's secret con-
claves were well and truly exposed, and it presumably ceased to
become an implement of high policy. But for twenty three years
Rockefeller and his cabal of high pressure C.F.R. executives had
been able to convene prestigious gatherings which from time to

time included past and future prime ministers of Western European countries, besides representatives of their few remaining royal houses, — all without a single news report going out through any of the communications media. It was an impressive reflection upon the monopoly power of this multi-millionaire chairman of the unofficial, unelected Fabian-inspired C.F.R., whose edicts had come to supersede the policy decisions of monarchs, presidents and their cabinets.

¶74.

THE POWER CAUCUS THAT WAS
FAILING THE WEST

There may not at this juncture be much raising of the blood pressure, particularly amongst our capitalist readers, even when it is realised that Kingmaker David had invited a few of the City's sworn enemies to his Bilderberg conferences, including the fallen idol Sir Harold Wilson and his radical sidekick Denis Healey. After all, one might say, these chaps, for all their revolutionary tendencies, had finally to settle down and function within the System, — and if their visits to Bilderberg taught them where the real authority lay, perhaps it wasn't such a bad thing for the stability of the Western World.

That would not have been such a bad argument either, if the Western World had continued to remain stable and united in face of the very real threat from the other side of the Iron Curtain. But all down through the years whilst the uncrowned King David was holding his prestigious get-togethers with power caucuses from the various states of the Atlantic community, the West kept getting caught on the wrong foot, — kept losing out in one crisis after another. As noted previously, the famed U.S. cavalry, whilst continuing to win all the celluloid engagements scripted and screened for it by Hollywood, was in real life getting badly roughed up by the local bums, and there were times when it seemed that its intelligence corps had gone over to the other side.

In the New Year of 1979 the four chief executive ministers of Britain, France, West Germany and the United States held a "summit" conference at Guadeloupe in the Caribbean. It was a pleasant sunny environment in which to escape temporarily from the rigours of frozen Europe, but the prepared hand-outs were no doubt calculated to persuade the electorates of the Western nations that the discussions held, and the decisions taken, would be of sufficient importance to justify both the expense and the absence from their own capitals.

So what did they talk about in that sub-tropical environment? Economics, no doubt! Means of alleviating the recession and improving world trade! But they were also expected to be deeply involved in matters of defence. Three of the four nations represented at Guadeloupe were partners in the NATO Alliance, and in view of the vast strides being taken by Soviet Russia to arm both herself and her satellites in the Warsaw Pact, it could be assumed that they would want to assess their joint situation vis-à-vis the only probable adversary.

A newspaper columnist, subsequently reporting on the conference to his readers back home in an ice-bound United Kingdom, suggested that for all the sunshine and the tropical luxuriance of that holiday island, the four leaders had not truly relaxed in enjoyment of their surroundings because *"their talk was of the doom weapons targeted by the Russians on British and European cities"*.

¶75. THE DREADFUL RECORD OF HENRY KISSINGER

How about that? Bit of a shock for the Rip Van Winkles who fell complacently asleep in the days when America was reckoned to have the Soviet Union ringed with ballistic missile bases covering all areas of military and industrial importance. In the missile crisis of 1962 for instance, when John F. Kennedy called Kruschev's bluff in the matter of the Cuban rocket sites, he bluffed successfully because the cards, — and the preponderance of weaponry, — were heavily stacked in his favour.

So what had happened during the intervening sixteen years to upset that favourable balance? *Doom weapons targeted upon British and European cities!* Somehow that just did not seem merely to recognise the Russians' right to mount some kind of credible reprisal. It seemed to infer that they had stolen a march, — that they had managed to achieve an advantage in this deadliest of war games, — and that the West had found itself in a position of terrifying inadequacy.

Rear Admiral Chester Ward, in his massive study "Kissinger on the Couch", — written in conjunction with Phyllis Schlafly, — lays much of the blame on that globe-trotting Secretary of State who, firstly under Richard Nixon, and latterly under Gerald T. Ford, had become the virtual Supremo of America's foreign policy, defence and security. Ward states that when Kissinger assumed office, the United States had a strategic nuclear strike superiority over the Soviet Union of something between three and four to one. When he departed some eight years later, the whole strike capability of the Western Alliance had taken such a lurch backwards that there were *doom weapons targeted upon British and European cities.* For this the ebullient doctor was awarded the Nobel Peace Prize, the title of *the world's most indispensable man*, and the jet set's accolade as its most eligible bachelor. Much of this image-building, say Ward and Schlafly, was directly attributable to himself.

THE EROSION OF THIRD WORLD
¶76.   ALLEGIANCES

So Kissinger had come and gone, and the great nation he had been appointed to serve was now in such a state of paralysis and lost confidence that she was no longer fit to lead the alliance of Western peoples who for years had clustered securely under her banner. All right for the French! Under that stubborn autocrat Charles de Gaulle, they had seen what was coming years before, and had made their own dispensations. But bedazzled by Harold MacMillan's "special relationship", — and particularly under Socialist Governments, — the British had slavishly followed the American line to the point of abject humiliation and beyond.

What also of that multiplicity of Third World peoples who, due to their own economic and military weakness, had to be on the winning side regardless? We have seen the horrific retribution meted out to South Vietnam when American nerves failed, and the activities of the *lemmus Americanus* sapped the national will to protect vital positions in Asia. One of President Carter's early gambits was to start negotiations for handing the strategic Panama Canal over to the Communist-controlled Panamanian Republic, and in some of the more volatile South American countries, where governments had sometimes changed along with the seasons, there were new-found doubts about either the will or the capability of the U.S.A. to sustain its protégés in the face of revolutionary undercurrents stirred up by a resurgent Cuba.

When an elderly Moslem cleric, from his enforced exile in Paris, finally succeeded in toppling the mighty Shah of Iran with his massive stockpile of sophisticated American arms, – and the Carter administration welshed on their ally at the worst psychological moment, – the message got home to all those anti-communist governments across the globe who had blindly pinned their faith upon the sturdy protection and benign approval of capitalist America. John Wayne was dead. The symbol of the big guy with a gun on his hip, ready to see justice and fair play and to defend his buddies, had passed away. The new America would rat on its friends in times of trouble, – and woo even its most implacable enemies, – all in the name of *rapprochement* or *détente*, or whatever other gem of *nuspeak* terminology was dreamed up as a euphemism for the old-fashioned double-cross.

As far as immediate matters were concerned, Carter would get the blame of course, – *he* would be the appointed fall guy, – the buffoon to outjester all other buffoons. But the real responsibility would lie with the executive directors of the C.F.R., that non-elected Fabian-inspired advisory body which, under David Rockefeller's chairmanship, had become the "invisible government" of the United States, and which had pushed and promoted Henry Kissinger till he became the right-hand man of presidents.

So what was the C.F.R. playing at? Even super-rich capitalists must surely take the view, if not from principle, at least from common sense, that in the matter of picking sides and developing alignments, you have to show good faith towards adherents and supporters to expect their co-operation in an emergency.

¶77.   FALL GUYS AND STRINGPULLERS

But now a nasty little thought starts tugging at the mind. Who are the pastmasters of the double-cross, the mental somersault and the stab in the back? Who can perform a volte-face whilst a more inhibited adversary is still considering whether to make a slight incline? What is the awful creed so ruthless and unprincipled that it can use people's very virtues with which to destroy them, and which is guided only by the dictum that the end justifies the means?

Uh-huh! Don't tell us. *We think we know.* That Lincoln School at Columbia University, where the youthful David Rockefeller got an early indoctrination in Fabianism through the "progressive" educational methods of John Dewey! But that was donkey's years ago, and since then the boy Rockefeller has risen to become one of the super-rich capitalists of New York's Wall Street. In fact the biggest in the business!

So who has been taken over by whom? Who are the fall guys and who are the stringpullers? Who is the kingpin and who are the stooges? In other words, has the Rockefeller business empire quietly taken over the Marxist-Fabian conspiracy? Or is it the latter which has now got a strangling hold on the nerve centre of monopoly capitalism?

Friend, if you knew the answer to that one, you would either be a candidate for high office in the alternative wing of the C.I.A., – or the target for a hit-man with a high velocity rifle.

DR HENRY KISSINGER

It was during the years of his
jet-shuttling diplomacy that the
U.S. cavalry stopped arriving in the
nick of time.

CHAPTER ELEVEN

¶ 78. The Prospectus of The Company

What now for the little chap with the city bowler, the striped suit and the rolled umbrella? The capitalist lemming! We kept him standing around all through the last chapter, and he must occasionally have wondered why he was there. But we did finally establish the sinister link between Big Monopoly Capitalism and Marxist-Fabian Collectivism, and since that is a conception which may take a bit of grasping, it's better to kick it around for a while till we get used to it.

And while we're at it, let's find a handy way of designating this weirdly assorted bunch of super-rich capitalist monopolists, Fabian gradualists, Marxists collectivists, global state internationalists and downright red revolutionaries who severally and collectively are working towards the destruction of our free Western society, — with the declared object of setting in its place a one-world authoritarian government which could not be other than tyrannical in nature, godless in its purpose and monolithic in its power structure, — which might, moreover, bearing in mind the present imbalance of strategic overkill, end up by being policed from a command computer in Moscow.

How to find a suitable collective name for such a complex and many-headed monster? Well it's been known for some of those maverick offshoots of the C.I.A., when seeking to identify their own umbrella organisation in contacts between agents, to refer to it simply as The Company. So THE COMPANY it shall be from now on, — and the collusion of those Big Big Mono-polists, Fabian-Marxists and Communist revolutionaries, wher-ever it is revealed, can be seen as the COMPANY prospectus. At least it should make the capitalist lemming feel a little more at home, as we proceed of necessity to shake some of the other conventions of his ordered world. You may hang your bowler and umbrella on the hat stand, old chap. Sit down and make yourself comfortable. We're coming to the point at last.

¶79. IMPORTANCE OF THE SOUTHERN AFRICA SYNDROME

So! having thrust ourselves right into the core of the matter, — and hopefully wriggled out again, — let us look anew at some of the peripheral evidence which cropped up in a pre-vious chapter in the context of Southern Africa.

No apology is offered for introducing the subject again, as it is the author's opinion that this is the make-or-break issue for the whole COMPANY prospectus. If they are ever going to over-reach themselves, it will be down there on the fringes of Capri-corn, where an obstinate white race still stands guard on the western approaches to the Indian Ocean, and where, north of the Limpopo, a remarkable degree of tolerance and under-standing between black and white races in pursuit of their own best interests is proving a sore and frustrating experience for the manipulators whose allotted task was to bring them safely into the internationalist net many years ago.

It was pointed out that much of the money used for financing subversion, terrorism and guerrilla wars in Southern Africa was provided by America's tax-exempt foundations, the largest of which being owned or controlled by the Rockefellers. It is also alleged that C.I.A. funds are being channelled through a variety of smaller organisations for a similar purpose, which means that the subversive movements are being surreptitiously subsidised by the American taxpayer.

Where there is overt recognition of these facts, it is generally justified as reflecting the influence of the black vote in American politics, as well as the extent to which the issue of *apartheid* has touched the mighty humanitarian heart of the great American public. But Americans as a race do not go on consciously working against their own best interests and it would be the height of purblind naivety to accept, for instance, that a motley collection of church welfarist, student and coloured and anti-discrimination groups have mounted and sustained the high-pressure campaign waged over a number of years to destroy the South African Government.

So what is really behind it?

THE ATTEMPT TO DEMONETISE GOLD

¶ 80.

It is now thirteen years since a former American lemming, who had decided to get out of the rodent race by using his brains instead of his group instincts, told the author that the key to the United States' assault on South Africa was a desire to lay hands on the gold-mining industry. This was shortly after word had got around about the master plan produced by the Carnegie Peace Foundation for a proposed military invasion of South Africa by United Nations forces. The logistics of that project seem grossly inadequate by today's standards, — less than a hundred thousand troops, several thousand warplanes and an estimated twenty to forty thousand casualties. But the abilities or deficiencies of the armchair strategists at the Carnegie Found-ation were much less significant than the heinous nature of the proposal to use U.N. auspices for an attack upon a member government. Here was documentary proof of aggressive inten-tions by an élite pressure group which obviously had the ear of the U.S. establishment. And as confirmation of the argument that gold was somehow a factor in this extremely hostile attitude, the Carnegie Endowment report, issued over the name of one Amelie C. Leiss, recommended a boycott on the yellow metal, along with a diminishing of its status as backing for Western World currencies.

Those with a knowledge of international financial and investment matters will have been able to observe only too clearly in recent years the extent to which the Carnegie Plan, —

or something similar, – has been put into operation. Praise be! we have not yet had the armed assault. (Whoever starts it is going to get a bloody nose in any case). But the consequences of America's anti-gold policy under successive adminstrations is just beginning to be felt by the taxpayer and the U.S. economy.

In the early nineteen sixties, even before the Carnegie report was circulated, the American Treasury was making strenuous efforts to maintain the price of gold at its pre-war value of 35 dollars per ounce, this despite the fact that there was inflation in every other commodity. The logic was that if this policy could be maintained, much of South Africa's gold-mining would become uneconomic through failure to recover its costs. By 1981, they predicted, only four of the existing mines on the Witwatersrand would still be operating, and the industry would be in a decline from which it could barely recover. This would facilitate the creation of a situation in which gold could be 'demonetised', and in its place the Americans proposed the substitution of a device called S.D.R.'s (or special drawing rights).

¶81.   DE GAULLE TO THE RESCUE

Now is the point where the capitalist lemming should climb out from behind his Financial Times and give us his undivided attention. S.D.R.'s! Paper gold! Do you realise that you nearly went right over the precipice on this one, old chap? Remember the cordial and uncritical reception which the financial community gave to this piece of monetary buffoonery, just because it had been proposed by the U.S. Treasury, and backed by the once mighty American dollar? Nowadays no one wants to talk too much about Special Drawing Rights. They are destined to meet the same fate as similar paper-backed securities down through history. But there was a time when the City of London and its acknowledged experts talked long and learnedly about this new fiddle as though it were the elixir.

It wasn't that our native chaps had suddenly lost all sense of financial rectitude, – just that, ever since the Mecca of the money game had floated across the Atlantic during the war, we had become accustomed to drooping our snouts, or doffing our bowlers, whenever Big Brother in Wall Street called the shots. And who was to know then that when we gave our unqualified approval to those phony S.D.R.'s, we had become acting unpaid servants of THE COMPANY, — where in their palatial dining room they occasionally have lemming cutlets for breakfast?

Yes, it was a near thing, wasn't it? Fortunately we had that stubborn old autocrat in the Elysée Palace to sort us out again. Old stiff-back Charles de Gaulle! Churchill's wartime Cross of Lorraine! The former expert on tank warfare probably knew as much about the money game as he did about diplomatic etiquette, but he was himself within the Rothschild financial orbit, and therefore not necessarily sympathetic to what the Rockefellers were planning in New York. In the years of his presidency, France resolutely and successfully defended the role of gold as an indispensable medium to the stability of international trade, and as a result a whole generation of capitalist lemmings were saved the pain and embarrassment of that final headlong rush over the precipice.

¶82.
THE PRESIDENT WHO TRIED
TO STOP THE TIDE

Once upon a time, away back in 1961, President John F. Kennedy had felt it incumbent upon himself to use the new technological breakthrough of an early Telstar broadcast for an announcement to the financial community that, come what might, gold would not be allowed to change its value. In our early Saxon history another absolute ruler stuck his throne on the sands of the Crouch Estuary and announced that he was going to stop the tide. As history records, the tide came in just the same.

So it was to prove with gold. Those who keep charts upon such things will confirm that in face of obduracy by the U.S. Treasury, a free market developed under which the price of the yellow metal traded upwards to 44 dollars an ounce, fell back under American counter-methods, and hung for a short period at a discount under the official par, before starting upon an irresistible upward surge which drove the pegged price completely out of sight. Gold hoards developed in France and the Far East, in Arab countries, and wherever there was unrest or currency instability.

In 1974 the price got to 180 dollars, by which time the American anti-gold lobby, in desperation, had pressurised their own administration into auctioning off part of the enormous hoard of bullion stored in Fort Knox, — not as a benefit to the hard-pressed American taxpayer, but under I.M.F. auspices, so that the premium profits would be creamed off into an ever-expanding international kitty.

That did the trick for a time. The price had dropped to just under 100 dollars by the beginning of 1977, and a number of South Africa's marginal mines, whose costs had continued to rise against a falling metal price, were assuming a very sickly appearance. Some of the older workings were closing shafts, others brought forward their dates for terminating production, and the predictions in the Carnegie Endowment plan were tending to look a little bit less exaggerated. The sharks hung about, watching for the impending wreck, and waiting to snap up the pieces.

COLLAPSE OF THE ONCE ALMIGHTY DOLLAR

¶83.

All this was taking place against a background of boycotts, threatened boycotts, and commercial, social and psychological pressures towards a disruption of contacts and trade. International companies which had strong links with South Africa were picketed by beatniks, student groups and Communist Front associations who had bought an odd hundred shares for the express purpose of blanketing general stockholders' meetings. Expensive adverts were taken in major American dailies propagandising against purchases of the gold kruggerand. South African sports teams got banned from the Olympics, the Davis Cup, cricket tests and rugby tours. They even had a chosen band of obsessive nitwits tramping round the golf links to barrack Gary Player. A hundred thousand lemmings, milling about frantically, knowing not what they were doing, — and even less about the consequences if they succeeded!

But some stories in this book *do* have a satisfactory ending. In spite of all the pressures, all the manipulation of bullion and commodity markets in the United States and Europe, the price of gold started to rise again. Sales by the U.S. Treasury increased, then increased again, till finally the Yanks were disposing of 750,000 ounces at a single auction. There soon came a day when even offerings of that magnitude made little difference to the persistent upward trend. Gold was fetching over 200 dollars an ounce by the end of 1978, and in the first half of 1979 the rise had accelerated till it hit 300 dollars by midsummer, — all this combined with a virtual collapse of the U.S. currency against strong European units such as the German mark, the Swiss franc and latterly the British pound.

In the money and bullion markets of the Western World, among the bowler hats, the rolled umbrellas and the pin-striped suits of the Exchanges, a battle had been won and lost, — a battle whose outcome might have significant consequences for the mass of humanity, even although not more than a fraction of one per cent of them would know what it was all about.

So! Still believe the moguls of Wall Street went through that titanic upheaval, devalued their currency and threw away a large slice of their nation's strategic reserve, just to appease the human rights crusaders or the Gays-against-apartheid Action Committee?

SUTTON'S BREATHTAKING
¶84.   SOLUTION

Frankly we might still all be a bit confused and wobbly-minded as to why they *did* do it, had it not been for a scholarly treatise which appeared in 1977, over the name of Antony C. Sutton, the American academic who in earlier years had so thoroughly investigated the enormous transfers of U.S. and European technology to Soviet Russia. Professor Sutton must be a formidable character upon whom to try out any form of intellectual sophistry. He tends to present his facts against an almost overwhelming mass of corroborative evidence, and he seldom over-emphasises his conclusions. So it appears that the only way in which a treacherous un-American Establishment can fight him is to pretend that he isn't there, — which is something they have managed to do very successfuly during those last six or seven years, so that the patriotic researches of this scholar-turned-investigator have received only a fraction of their merited publicity.

In his "War on Gold" Sutton makes an observation which should have been obvious enough to the rest of us, yet which seems to have escaped general notice until he gave it emphasis. This is to the effect that gold and gold-backed reserves impose a *discipline* which is totally unacceptable to the collectivist, the spendomaniac, the bureaucratic empire builder, the nationaliser and all that crazy gang of Marxist-Fabians whose plans for the distribution of wealth have always been frustratingly handicapped by the limitations on its creation. South Africa currently produces about two-thirds of the West's supply of newly mined gold, which is somewhat more than half of the total world supply. The second largest producer is Soviet Russia, with about twenty-nine per cent.

The argument goes that if one single power group could control both the South African sources and the Russian production as well, then with eighty per cent of the total world capacity in its hands, *it would have a stranglehold on international trade and the convertibility of currencies.* The notable thing about this hypothesis is that the high-flown talk in prestigious financial circles about phasing out and ultimately de-monetising gold is seen to have been an elaborate bit of kite-flying for the confusion of the lemmings, who might thus be persuaded to part with their holdings at a discount. The men who fought the war on gold with paper S.D.R.'s, and with every other cynical, psychological and propaganda trick in the book, did so with very clear minds as to their own required objective. After all, if you want to buy up a commodity cheaply, — and you start with a complete absence of moral scruples, — it is worthwhile persuading the holders, as well as other intending purchasers, that they are operating in a declining market, with an ultimate fall off in demand.

That, in Professor Sutton's learned submission, has been the true motive for the multi-million dollar campaign to wreck the South African economy. With regard to the eternally breathtaking assumption that there can from time to time be close affinity of purpose between Big Capitalism on the one hand and Communist Collectivism on the other, — a conception which so many orthodox Western thinkers find it very difficult to accept, — Sutton was obviously able to reach his conclusions by leisurely stages, having already put on record his researches into Wall Street financing for the Bolshevik Revolution of 1917.

A SIMPLE MATTER OF ORTHODOX FINANCE

¶ 85.

Some thirty years earlier than Sutton, a Scottish physician who delved deeply into the enigmas and the myths which dominate our attitudes to social and economic systems, was providing material which will help us to span the ideological void. In his "Human Ecology", published by William MacLellan in 1949, Dr. Thomas Robertson points out that despite all the savagery of the October Revolution and its aftermath, despite the killings and the purges, the slave camps and the political trials, the total expurgation of private capital and the mass confiscation of property, Soviet economists did not in the end achieve anything approaching a new financial system. *They merely adapted the techniques and methods of capitalism to their own peculiar needs.* They did this as much out of necessity as from any lapse of ideological fervour, because they had quickly realised that they could not revive their wartorn and prostrate empire without technical and material assistance from abroad, — and that would not be made available except on the terms of orthodox finance. Robertson maintains in fact that, through the Gosbank, Soviet Russia had re-established an orthodox banking and financial system as early as 1921.

If at this stage we now adopt the mathematician's trick of substituting symbols, we might come to a clearer conception of something which the initiates have understood all along. Suppose for the term *Big Capitalism* we substitute *Money Power*, we see

123

at once, on the basis of Thomas Robertson's researches, that our Western-orientated conception of likes and opposites is no longer valid.

We have tended, have we not, to look upon capitalism, — aye and latterly upon its illegitimate and unprepossessing offspring Big Monopoly Capitalism, — as the champion and the standardbearer for our entire collection of Western values? Free speech! Free association! Freedom of movement within our own country and those of friendly neighbours! Justice and equality before the law! The right to criticise and change governments and institutions, — to retain and bequeath the fruits of our labours! Within these broad principles, — and with due recognition of the wealth-creating agencies and organisms, — the privilege and the responsibility of ensuring that all our people are provided with a reasonable standard of life and opportunity! Might that be taken as a fair assessment of our expectations under modern welfarist capitalism, — and incorporating all its monopolist and supra-national offshoots? Is that what we shall be fighting to defend if we ever get ourselves into another large-scale shooting war? And if it is, do we give the same self-sacrificial allegiance to our defence of the Money Power as we undoubtedly would in preservation of our treasured Western values?

WHERE THE CONFLICTING IDEOLOGIES
¶86.   COME TOGETHER

According to Dr. Robertson, the two ideals are not synonymous. Or putting it another way, the Money Power, having substituted itself for liberal capitalism, would simply not be worthy of our sacrifices. Why? Because in the sorry history of our twentieth century from 1917 onwards it has concerned itself more with the procedures and the protocol of *orthodox finance* than with the freedom of the soul and the decencies of life. The banking centres of Europe and America may at first have shown genuine alarm at the excesses and the social upheavals of the Bolshevik era, but they soon settled down to work with the Soviets when they found that they could provide them with long-term credits at satisfactory rates of interest.

It did not really matter how many innocent wretches were languishing in the Lubianka Prison if the bankers felt they had an accommodation which would keep the new Union of Soviet Republics within their sphere of influence.

So are we now getting closer to an understanding of this nigh incredible collusion of interests between Big Money Capitalism in New York and Communist Collectivism in Moscow, as they jointly finance and foment revolution in those regions of the Earth where thus far neither of them has achieved a satisfactory degree of penetration?

We are not at this stage enunciating a theory or evolving a hypothesis, in an effort to dream up skulduggery and melodrama out of the normal interplay of inter-state relations. As we have learned with Professor Antony Sutton, the skulduggery and the cloak-and-dagger situations already exist. With him it was mainly a matter of gleaning facts from a variety of sources, checking and collating them, putting them into a framework, then satisfying himself that that framework corresponded with what was happening in the world around him. No one can totally negate or refute the evidence which this former research fellow of the Hoover Institute has brought to public notice. Some of it comes from U.S. State Department files, some from official compilations of statistical data, some from authenticated commercial records. It is there. It happened. It was factually recorded at the time of each occurrence. All it needed was someone of sufficient scholarship, pertinacity and dedication to put the whole picture together.

And nowhere is that picture emerging with greater clarity than in the context of Southern Africa, where wealthy tax-exempt American foundations and maverick agencies of the C.I.A. are providing funds, expertise and agents on the ground for the incitement of civil strife and bloody revolution. In this they are co-ordinating their efforts with groups and organisations which obtain their inspiration and their ideology from the other side of the Iron Curtain. It is just another of those situations where the onlooker wonders which of the unheavenly twins is hoping finally to control and manipulate the other.

They would both of course be just that bit less effective if it were not for the lemmings, that starry eyed assortment of irrepressible do-gooders, civil rights emancipators, trade union fellow travellers, anti-apartheid crusaders and inveterate meddlers who have a solution to everyone's problems except their own. Be it seen from the foregoing pages whose cause they are really serving when they march and demonstrate, stage boycotts, and commit both their energy and their finances to organisations with high-sounding names which turn out to be Communist fronts tactically planted for the enticement and the seduction of the unwary.

¶87. PEOPLE WHO STAND GUARD ON OUR LIFELINES

Our Western society is in a mess. But we do justice, neither to ourselves nor to the lesser endowed nations of Southern Africa, if we erode the moral fibre, the confidence and the resistance capability of the one race which can guarantee us a breathing space, a continuing source of strategic minerals, and friendly monitoring of the sea lanes round the Cape of Good Hope.

Then what about *apartheid?* Well for a start, it means *separate development,* — not racism, or repression, or institutionalised violence, or the eternal social and economic subjugation of one race by another. It was adopted in South Africa some thirty years ago because a white minority saw it then as the only means by which they could preserve their culture and their identity. Already the irritants and the petty humiliations attendant upon *apartheid* are being progressively eliminated, will tend to disappear and become things of the past as the various races develop an interdependent relationship.

It is a delicate process of evolution, — not at all assisted by blatant and ill-informed external criticisms, — and certainly not benefited or accelerated by the massive subversive activities of the American C.I.A., who, if we are to accept the findings of Professor Sutton, are less concerned about the dignity of man and the welfare of peoples than about control of the gold-mining industry, which, once theirs, would give THE COMPANY and its Marxist associates a stranglehold upon the world's markets and convertibility of currencies.

Capitalist lemmings please note!

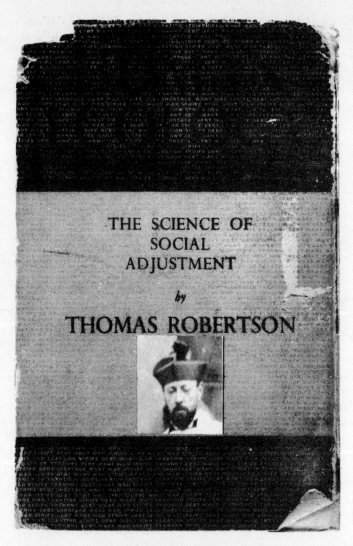

THE SCIENCE OF
SOCIAL
ADJUSTMENT

by

THOMAS ROBERTSON

DR THOMAS ROBERTSON

Author of "Human Ecology —
the Science of Social Adjustment"

CHAPTER TWELVE

¶88. **Leading Up To Some Proposals**

Well! now that we've been through the wringer and back again, one wonders how many of the cynical souls who started out are still with us, — and how many are still cynical.

After all, it must seem a bit of an upturn, with THE COMPANY financing and fomenting revolution whilst sitting on top of the heap over there in Wall Street. Upsets the whole foundation of the ideological struggle and the class war, doesn't it? I mean, who can you *trust* any more, — even to be beastly when it's jolly well expected of him? We set out to make a study of subversion, — and subversives eyed us warily, for *they* were what we were meant to be *against*. Now it appears there might just be something of interest in it *for* them as well. Either they learn some tricks and contrivances which are new to their repertoire, — or they go through an agonising reappraisal as they realise for whom they have been working.

Makes you spit, doesn't it, even at the very suggestion that THE COMPANY might have a vested interest in all those deserving revolutionary causes to which you have devoted your energies and your idealism? When you rallied and demonstrated, stormed the barricades, stoned the police, — connived at a total disintegration of civil order, — it was these capitalist moneybags, right there at the back of the Establishment bandwagon, whom you reckoned to be the real enemy of the classless revolution. You might not get at them directly by bashing coppers' helmets

129

or joining Rent-a-picket for the next confrontation on the industrial scene, but it was comforting to feel that whilst you were
still too distant to hit them over the head, you could at least hit
them through their pockets. Besides, it was all building up inevitably and inexorably towards that glorious day when the workers
would throng into the streets, when the acknowledged bastions
of wealth and privilege would be battered down, when the
exploited would rise against the exploiters throughout the length
and breadth of the land, — and when the ghost of Father Lenin
would hover around expectantly to see the last capitalist hanged
by his own rope.

But *would* he hang? And if he did hang, would he be the
last? After the disclosures of Thomas Robertson and Antony
C. Sutton, can we really be sure about anything? Is this what
the fervour of revolution is all about, — building a brave new
federalist world in which the bankers would be re-establishing
the structures of *orthodox finance* before the blood had stopped
running in the gutters?

¶89.   EXPLOITING CLASS RIGIDITIES

The Scottish vernacular poet Hugh MacDiarmid was wont
to declare that he "must be a Bolshevik before the revolution,"
but that he would cease to be one immediately Communism
took over. Unlike the lemmings whom he led and encouraged in
his lifetime, MacDiarmid suspected what lay at the end of that
last long headlong rush over the precipice, but with characteristic
perversity he preferred to let the rest of the swarm find out for
themselves. *His* moment of redemption was to be *their* moment
of truth, and of course it would all be tragically much too late.
The misguided idealism which had done so much to subvert our
own traditional values would be cast in futile opposition against
the new authoritarianism, only to be crushed as the mensheviks
were crushed, or the Hungarians in the carnage of Budapest.

You and I, having learned a thing or two from such macabre
episodes, can have little concern for the shattered illusions of
the Leninists, the Trotskyists, and all those other fanatical
adherents of red revolution who would pull down our existing

society without much idea of what to put in its place. The militant reds are no longer the menace that they used to be. The danger lies with many millions of steadfast, though lesser committed souls who eschew the violent solution at all times, yet whose unsuspecting compliance with today's prevailing trends could still usher in a collectivist tyranny, — with or without the trauma of national surrender or the threat of nuclear war.

These are the people whose instinctive class and group loyalties make for the permanent entrenchment of policies and attitudes within the political system. In the past the Fabians have manipulated them to bring about gradual change. Now THE COMPANY, with its impressive stranglehold upon the mass communications industry, is busy shaping their ideas and their aspirations to fit a new world order in which nations and nationalities, traditions and ethnic differences, individuality of thought and action, morality and religious belief, respect and remembrance of our heroic past as well as patriotic endeavour for our present and future, are all frowned upon as reactionary tendencies in the thrust towards global conformity.

Do you like having your ideas and your opinions moulded and shaped like a blob of clay on a potter's rotary? Does it worry you that those two diametrically opposed ideologies, Monopoly Capital and Communist Collectivism, might indeed be different outward manifestations of the same financial mechanism, — and that their clandestine collusion could progressively narrow our options to go on living as free democratic peoples for the indefinite future?

Can you be shocked out of your social and political prejudices, so that you may look with different eyes upon your fellow countrymen, — whether as workers or managers, trade unionists or entrepreneurs, stiff necks, rubber necks, cloth caps, bowler hats, aristos or devotees of the common man? Is it possible to have a realignment of our basic tenets and antagonisms, — a coming together of all those decent and honourable souls who want to sustain and uplift our national consciousness, — a closing of the ranks against those who would fain destroy it?

¶90.   THE PASSPORT TO
                  PREFERMENT

The revelation in the autumn of 1979, that the fourth man
in the MacLean-Burgess-Philby spy imbroglio was Sir Anthony
Blunt, Surveyor of the Queen's pictures, surely disposed of any
fanciful delusions that Marxism and its associated treacheries
were in any way the sole resort of the downtrodden and the
underprivileged. Blunt was preparing for the life of an English
upper class academic when he met the homosexual Guy Burgess
at Cambridge University in the nineteen-thirties, and by his own
admission he and a group of other top-drawer intellectual young
scarecrows thenceforth allowed themselves to be persuaded that
the only way to defeat the Nazis was to become Marxists, and
offer their services to Communist Russia. Apparently there was
no particular secret about this commitment of a significant
segment of the Cambridge intelligentsia to a foreign power who
might one day become a dangerous enemy. Donald MacLean
and Kim Philby were also acknowledged members of the clique,
and in the climate of the times this had not prevented them from
being appointed to high posts in diplomacy and counter-intelligence, from which they were able to deliver much vital security
and technological information to their new ideological masters
in Moscow.

Neither did it prevent Anthony Blunt himself from being
recommended for a key position in M.I.5 during the early stages
of the Second World War. By his own testimony, the unknown
official who gave him the vital recommendation was well aware
of his Marxist sympathies, and it would be naive to presume that
he did not know he was planting a potential Russian spy in
Britian's most exclusive security service. In the aftermath Establishment apologists have endeavoured to explain this away as a
misguided application of the "old boy" and "old school tie"
network, but for those who have come to understand the true
allegiance and ultimate ambition of the British Fabians, there is
nothing strange in a situation where university dons, a future
Surveyor of the Queen's pictures, Foreign Office diplomats and

132

highly placed recruitment officers of the counter-intelligence services should all be more or less fanatical devotees of the ghastly creed which even then had turned the Russias into a massive prison house. Anthony Blunt was not selected in spite of his Marxist sympathies. *They were in fact his passport to preferment.*

HOW MANY MORE ESTABLISHMENT TRAITORS?

¶91.

It was claimed that Blunt had been useless to either the Russians or the British authorities for some fifteen to twenty years before his public exposure. Some emphasis was placed upon the fact that he had continued in his privileged appointment within the royal household at Buckingham Palace even after the full extent of his treacheries had been revealed to the British Secret Service, and in the House of Commons there were several critical questions from the Labour benches as M.P's wondered how one who had so grievously betrayed the security of the state should have been allowed to go on living his comfortable bourgeois existence, totally without restriction or punishment. But the obvious concern of Labour's crypto-Marxists was to see that the publicity given to the Blunt affair did not spark off a witch hunt which might flush out more Establishment traitors. They at least had gone to the core of the matter, — that the Blunt-MacLean-Burgess espionage agency had been out of business for a quarter of a century. The KGB most likely had a new generation of collectivist-minded paranoics strategically situated in the right places, and it behove their loyal fellow travellers in the Commons to keep the spotlight facing where we had been, rather than where we were going.

You and I, of course, do now have a fair conception of the complex organism which promotes potential traitors and subversives into positions of peculiar power. We know that its place-men are just as likely to be top-drawer academics as shop stewards on the factory floor, — and we are circumspect enough to assume that the self-perpetuating oligarchy which selected, — and subsequently protected, — MacLean and Burgess, might

still be presiding over vital areas of our administrative
bureaucracy.

LABOUR AND THE
¶92.   CLASS WAR

So despite its proletarian overtones, Marxism is not a
working class philosophy at all. Yet through its links with
Fabian-Socialism it has managed to persuade several generations
of organised workers and their elected political representatives
that it is both the religion and the philosophy of the future. Do
we agree that it is nothing of the kind, — that it is only one facet of
the monolithic power structure which will be imposed upon us
if through wars and rumours of war, recurring economic crises
and nuclear blackmail, we finally allow ourselves to be cajoled
into a One World authoritarian state?

Labour, — and Labour politicians — have no right to go on
perpetuating the outworn dogmas of the class war in an age when
class is no longer an obstacle to advancement or opportunity, —
and when this, along with a hundred other hoary old shibboleths
and prejudices, is being used as a tactic to confuse and divide us,
— to dissuade us from taking the steps which will become
essential to our national survival. We are not by any means at a
dead end as we see the economies of the Western World drift into
just another of those all too familiar recessions, — as *orthodox
finance* responds by jacking up interest rates and the cost of
consumer credit, as thousands are forced out of paid employment, not because there is no work to be done, no need to be
served, but because the industrial wage-cost structure has been so
distorted by fiscal manipulations and trade union protectionism
that the individual employers, companies and corporations
within the system are forced to restrict output and shed workers
to retain, or regain, their own financial viability. All this and the
advent of the silicon chip!

¶93.   THE ROBOT REVOLUTION

So what is the way forward? Well in 1976 an American
scientist-technologist called James S. Albus published a book

called "People's Capitalism". which, as he appropriately indicated in his sub-title, was an effort to anticipate "the economics of the robot revolution". Through his study of cerebellar mechanisms and their application to robot construction and control, Albus has an insight into those sweepingly advanced technologies which came into being with the computer, and he states with some confidence that the process has now become regenerative,that machines will go on to build even more sophisticated machines, and ultimately acquire the capability to be taught behaviour patterns, such as is now the sole prerogative of the human brain.

This can become either a nightmare of science horror fiction or the pathway to an exciting new future, depending upon the morality of those who guide and control it. Fortunately James Albus is not only a robot-technologist, he is also a Christian believer of simple faith and moving piety, and his struggle to reconcile those truly frightening technological developments with the immortality of the human soul has brought forth from him an enunciation of one of those blinding truths which governments and vested interests and fossilised institutions will for ever try to keep hidden from us, just because their realisation and implementation could be politically or sectarially inexpedient.

Setting the scenario for the revolution which has to come, with robots building robots, and the new computerised robots learning behaviour patterns which will enable them to fulfil most of the productive processes currently operated by human labour in factories, Albus asks himself who will own those incredibly complex machines as they dispense with the work potential of millions. Will they fall into the hands of a small number of multi-national giant corporations who alone will have the vast capital resources necessary to develop the expertise and lay down the automated production lines upon which those computerised dogsbodies will ultimately perform? And if they do, what means will be adopted to distribute the wealth which has been so effortlessly created?

Forget here those Luddite concepts of a previous century,

when enraged workers destroyed the new machinery which seemed to be depriving them of their jobs. Sophisticated robot technology exists. It can neither be discarded nor forgotten. If it is not adopted in this country or in Europe or the United States, it will be monopolised by rival industrial giants like Japan or Soviet Russia, and will then be used against us either militarily or economically, so that we emerge as the new under-developed nations of the twenty-first century.

So it is impossible, — or unthinkable, — to go back. We are impelled by our own survival instincts to go forward, — but as Christians and emancipators, not as drones and superfluous human flotsam which the computer age has made expendable. Then how do we humanise the robot revolution, so that it can become an enriching experience for all mankind, rather than profit and aggrandisement for the very few?

¶94.
SHARING THE PROCEEDS OF THE NEW TECHNOLOGY

Albus notes that despite the fact that his native land is renowned throughout the world as the bastion of capitalism and free enterprise, only a minority of Americans can claim to be capitalists in the accepted sense of the word, in that they are remunerated, either wholly or in part, by profit on their investments. The great bulk of his fellow citizens are wage and salary earners, living week to week or month to month from one pay cheque to another, and dependent upon the whims and requirements of the labour market and the various service industries to provide them with the wherewithal for a civilised existence. This is equally so in Britain, where the early stages of automation are already drawing an anguished response from the trade unions, and statisticians produce graphs to indicate that a proportion of the children at school now may never find remunerative work in their entire lifetimes.

It is the psychosis induced by the silicon chip and its associated technology which has led to the premature demand for work sharing and a drastic shortening of the working week, tendencies which merely aggravate our current state of industrial debility as unit costs are inflated by the under-employment of expensive buildings and machinery, and we lose more and more of our market spread to less inhibited competitors abroad. If by union hysteria and management futility this process is allowed to continue, we shall simply end up importing other people's unemployment, whilst having no means to remedy our own.

Now comes the blinding truth. Like all historic, epoch-making concepts from the wheel to the development of the steam engine, it is so simple that it might for ever have eluded our notice. This is what it says; *that with the advent of the robot revolution, wages and salaries can no longer be regarded as the only means of distributing the nation's wealth.* Hear that! you union secretaries and shop stewards who are in the forefront of all the strikes and demonstrations to resist shop closures and reduced manning levels. There could be a good and satisfying life for many of your erstwhile members away from the dust and the hubbub of the factory floor. In earlier ages the drive to industrialise, denuded the countryside, and in our own generation it has lowered the quality of life by making all those little less important jobs unremunerative, or by forcing them off the market altogether as a result of minimum wage regulations. A community which can make fullest use of the available technology to produce the bulk of its manufactured wealth need not, indeed must not, have an unacceptable proportion of its citizens in poverty, or living off some form of national dole. And to avoid this, we must get away from the concept of institutionalised work and salary earning quotas as the only means of ensuring that the average man and woman gets his or her share of an expanding GNP.

James S. Albus suggests a dividend, created by an investment corporation which he calls the National Mutual Fund, and which, sponsored and guaranteed by Government, would take a major share in all the vast capitalisation programmes which would be necessary to get the robot technology industries into production. Its shareholders would be the nation itself, every man, woman and child therein, — and as an increasing proportion of the national wealth was produced by the direct

137

application of a diminishing workforce, an apparatus would be available to spread the surpluses around for the benefit of all. With typical Yankee optimism and enthusiasm, Albus projects his idea into the first quarter century of robotisation, and reckons that by this time the individual dividend could have reached six thousand dollars per annum.

	MAJOR DOUGLAS AND
¶95.	SOCIAL CREDIT

A national dividend! The concept was not entirely new. It had been mooted, written about and actively canvassed in the nineteen-twenties by Major C.H.Douglas, a Scottish engineer who is recognised as the founder of the Social Credit Movement. Douglas came into the public eye when he started articulating his concern about a financial and economic system which persistently failed to match purchasing power with the national capacity to produce. As he saw it in those years after the First World War, there were human needs which went unsatisfied whilst both hands and factories were idle which possessed the means of fulfilling such needs. Financiers and economists assured him that it was all a complex business of depressing demand to match the supply of money available, but Douglas, being of a scientific and an enquiring mind, was not convinced. His researches took him to the fundamental creation of money itself, and much of what he uncovered was subsequently published in his "The Monopoly of Credit" in 1931.

He decided that the shortfall between production capacity and purchasing power was explained by the orthodox Treasury device of *debt financing*, whereby a government, to fund its commitments, borrowed money from the banking system, sometimes at substantial rates of interest. This money was not banknotes and silver coin, as you and I understand it, but was simply a *debit* entry in the banker's ledger. It was the bank which had created the credit, and it had done so without the realisation of a comparable sum in assets.

Douglas felt that the perpetuation of this procedure over a period of time would indicate that most of the country's tangible wealth was mortgaged to the banking system, and that the strain of servicing this gathering mountain of debt was denying the people that access to better living standards and greater leisure which they might otherwise enjoy as a spin-off from improved technology. His own proposal was that governments should simply take back the device of creating credit into their own hands, and that they should then enter into commitments only to the extent that physical resources of labour and materials were within their control. Out of this amended system of raising credit rather than financing debt, he reckoned that the Exchequer would emerge with a surplus that could from time to time be distributed in the form of a national dividend, which doubtless would go some way towards the shortfall in purchasing power that had aroused his curiosity in the first place.

¶ 96. WAR AS A FINANCIER'S STRATAGEM

It is recorded that when C.H. Douglas's theories were initially made public in 1918-19, they aroused a considerable amount of interest and speculation in the daily press of that time. But subsequently the subject was banned, — he was given the now only too familiar *silent treatment*, — from which it may be concluded that his proposals had engendered a certain amount of displeasure, even alarm, in highly influential quarters.

There used to be a popular song entitled *Money is the Root of all Evil*. In choosing to investigate the money system, Douglas believed that he had gone to the very heart of an involved conspiracy, and was not unduly surprised by anything that happened to him or his work in consequence. He was convinced that the prevailing orthodoxy of debt financing meant recurrent slumps and crises, and in the ultimate would lead to war. He forecast the Second World War as a direct result of the Great Depression of 1931, and some of his observations on the international skulduggery which was allegedly practised to protect the interests of those banking empires makes balanced reading against the machinations, manipulations, betrayals, atrocities and mass terror tactics which we in this modern age feel inclined to associate with THE COMPANY. It seems that certain things have scarcely changed at all.

But the bright contribution made in recent years by James Albus means that at least some of Douglas's ideas could be resurrected and forced into practice by technological change. *He* saw the surpluses accruing from his proposed financial reforms as a sort of national dividend. Albus wants his fellow citizens to benefit from increased prosperity through their share in his National Mutual Fund. But the one inescapable reality which in due course will have to be faced by bankers and politicians alike is the fact that *under the robot revolution, wages and salaries can no longer be regarded as the sole means of distributing wealth.*

THAT DISCARDED TAX-CREDIT
¶97.   SCHEME

How now! you Labour democrats who concern yourselves with the politics of the common man? How are *you* going to face up to the challenge of the robot revolution? By a somewhat despairing endorsement of the union demands for work sharing and shorter production weeks, — or by some imaginative concept such as has been introduced by James Albus in his "People's Capitalism"? Labour had the embryo of Albus's idea in its grasp when it inherited Anthony Barber's tax-credit scheme in 1974, but threw it out before it could go into practice.

Under the Barber proposals the entire workforce would be registered for income tax as normal, and those whose wages or other remuneration were above the tax exemption line would pay the going rate. But those whose earnings came below the line were intended to receive a tax credit, which would be proportionately greater the further the individual's wage returns fell below the accepted minimum.

This scheme has been a talking point for many years in the United States under the name of "negative" income tax, and it has been obvious to the author for some time that a modified and extended version would do much to alleviate the problems of the poverty gap, — as well as the much more intractable

140

situation which arises when a man on social security avoids all attempts to entice him back on to the labour market because the wages he is offered for working are only marginally better than he can get by drawing the dole. Put him on a tax credit rota, and he will *want* to be employed because the amount paid to him in "negative" tax by the revenue will have increased the attractiveness of work over idleness.

The other disincentive to employment which could be eliminated by this device is the insistence on a relatively high minimum wage, even for modest duties of a menial nature. It is this shortsighted measure of union protectionism which has driven so many of the hewers of wood and drawers of water from the labour market, thereby preventing many a simple soul from finding congenial employment at his own level of output and activity, and incidentally denying us the humble services he was both willing and able to perform. Put that harmless fellow on the tax-credit scheme also, — he'll enjoy working for his money, instead of collecting social security, — and the extra that comes through his "negative" assessment from the revenue will make it that much more worthwhile.

Add on the vast army of small-time tax dodgers, cash-in-the-hand casuals, and moon-lighters who are technically on the dole. When they learn that the State can occasionally pay a dividend, as well as exacting penalties, many of them may just choose to be registered, — with a corresponding diminution of their need or their opportunity to swindle the social security system.

¶ 98.   EVOLVING A DISTRIBUTIVE
                         MACHINERY

It may be that administrative experience in operating such a scheme is absolutely essential against the day when the robot industries become capable of producing the nation's needs with a direct involvement from only a fraction of the available workforce. At that stage fiscal machinery must be on hand to ensure that those whose employment prospects take them outside of the technological complexes have an inalienable right to participate on a *pari passu* basis in the monetary surpluses accumulated. So for a humble beginning, let's look again at Anthony Barber's discarded tax credit proposals. They might just evolve into something resembling Major Douglas's national dividend, or James Albus's National Mutual Fund. The advocates of orthodox finance will *take the mickey*, of course, — but we have begun to suspect, have we not, that there might just be a fundamental fallacy in all their pretentious reasoning?

Talk to me about such matters, O working man's politician! Talk to me first about the creation of wealth, and then the means of its distribution. Talk about higher earnings, dividend sharing, the right of the worker always to belong, always to participate in what he has helped to create. Talk about better living standards, and more leisure achieved with less effort through increased technology. Talk to me about such things and I will support you, — as will many a hard-nosed capitalist whom you have customarily regarded as being on the other side of the divide.

But revert to the nineteenth century dogmas of Karl Marx, the guff and the polemics of international socialism, — and I will know that you have gone back to working for THE COMPANY.

CHAPTER THIRTEEN

¶99. How The Yanks Got Anaesthetised

The Americans are statistically a literate people. Every year they print, publish, buy and read an enormous quantity of newspapers, plus a dazzling assortment of glossy and coloured magazines which treat in copious detail with every conceivable subject from home decorating to the habits of the Hudson Valley wood louse. Conservationists shudder at the acreage of virgin forest which might go to produce even a few issues of the New York Times.

Even so, Americans in the mass remain almost totally disinformed, — particularly upon the matters which concern their status as a super-power and acknowledged leader of the Western democratic world. When they finally got into World War II, many of them were quietly comforted by the thought that whatever happened, it would mean the end of the British Empire, — and in the strategic re-deployments and upheavals of the post-war years, positively nothing that happened east of Suez or south of Capricorn was going to distract them from the golf course or the ball game, or what went on in their hometown back streets. Most of the foreign crises seemed to be brewing just about the time when they were about to elect a new president, and in the hullabaloo and razzamatazz of domestic politics those Yanks sure showed the outside world that they knew how to fix their priorities.

They were in the throes of just another presidential

143

JAMES S. ALBUS
Author of "People's Capitalism"

spellbinder as Sir Anthony Eden was fuming over what he considered to be Egyptian bad faith in the Canal Area, and when the British and French finally invaded Suez in the autumn of 1956, President Eisenhower lost nothing in votes or popularity by ditching his wartime allies to the extent that their stabilising influence in the Middle East was permanently impaired. Ten to fifteen years later it was Vietnam that was catching the headlines, and now a lot of good clean American boys were getting killed or wounded in the paddy fields of the Mekong Delta, trying to retrieve a position which the same likeable Ike had thrown away when he allowed the French *paras* to be sacrificed at Dien Bien Phu.

Still the average American citizen persisted with his fuzzy and derogatory impression of what went on beyond the vast oceans that stretch eastwards of the Statue of Liberty and westwards of the Golden Gate Bridge in California. He knew that when trouble came those days it generally came from foreign parts, and he reckoned that things would only settle down when they had finally got rid of poverty and colonialism, and taught the under-developed world how to drive tractors, chew gum and operate hotdog stands. To this end he dug deep in his pockets, and gave generously of his tax dollars to buy food for the starving millions of Asia, and guns for the liberation armies of Southern Africa.

It was all with a great sense of detachment, as though those coolies and black dervishes were denizens of another planet, whose agonisings and occasional violent eruptions could do little to upset the tenor of American existence. The Russian menace was real enough, but the Soviets too were waging a crusade against exploitation and colonialism. It was a theme on which the two super powers could sure work together, and if *détente* could somehow preserve the integrity of the continental United States, it was just too bad that the outermost peripheries of the NATO Alliance became somewhat fragile, or some of the coloured races south of Capricorn whom they had been freeing of colonialism ended instead under repressive Marxist dictatorships.

145

Americans could accept those portentous happenings with equanimity because it was all beautifully rationalised and explained away in their daily newspapers. It seemed in this post-Cold War era that the political complexion of the regime was immaterial so long as their business men and their bankers could trade with it. And all that old stuff about preserving the Third World from Communist conquest was out of date since the Soviets and the U.S.A. started allocating their respective spheres of hegemony. Latterly with the C.I.A. apparently encouraging terrorist and revolutionary groups against the established pro-Western governments in volatile regions of South America, there began to be some confusion as to whose hegemony was which, but it was still a long way from Madison Avenue or Times Square, and folks acknowledged that their agents and representatives down there were bound to be having their problems.

¶100.   DITCHING THE SHAH OF IRAN

During all this period the Americans' most dependable ally in the Middle East was the Shah of Iran. The increased extraction from his vast oilfields had helped the U.S.A. to recover from the oil crisis of 1973-74, and whilst the other Arab states were playing politics with their mineral resources, the Shah had never wavered in his contractual obligations to deliver crude oil against the enormous purchases which he made from American business in the form of food, armaments, consumer and capital goods.

Even so, when his regime was racked by a general strike and politically motivated riots in the autumn of 1978, American attitudes to their faithful ally were somewhat equivocal. The Shah himself claimed afterwards that a US Air Force general who arrived in Teheran at the beginning of 1979 had been sent to depose him, and that it was American influence, exerted upon the chiefs of his powerful armed forces, which had prevented them from coming to his assistance when his throne was threatened. As the final humiliation, the announcement of his abdication was first made in Washington, not in Teheran, and a few days later he was forced into exile.

Thenceforth the country went into the throes of a fanatical

146

Islamic revolution, as a result of which parts of the United States suddenly ran short of motor spirit in the summer of 1979. It appeared that the co-operative, if now discredited Shah, had maintained a high rate of oil extraction, not only to pay for his military purchases, but also to finance a vast programme of development which he claimed would prepare the ancient Persian Empire for the advent of the twenty-first century. The new Khomeini regime, on the other hand, was intent on looking backwards rather than forwards, and having cancelled most of the outstanding military and development contracts, looked as if it might settle down to producing only as much crude as would be required for its own ongoing necessities, — which might not be a great deal, bearing in mind the Ayatollah's exhortations towards prayer and austerity.

A LEGACY OF UNPRINCIPLED DIPLOMACY

¶101.

The ditching of the Shah looked to have been a deliberate act of COMPANY policy, though in view of the resultant anarchy it must be difficult for ordinary mortals like you and me to fathom what they could hope to gain by it, — except perhaps another upheaval in the crude oil markets, where their own mammoth investments would appreciate accordingly. On the political side the withdrawal of support for their own protégé had embarrassed the Western World by creating yet another area of revolutionary turmoil, this time on the borders of the Soviet Union, — and since it was the sort of ploy they had been trying for years in Southern Africa, one could recognise the tactics without following through on the reasoning.

One did not even know whether the new Islamic regime was one which they hoped to control and manipulate, or whether events had simply got out of hand. According to the Shah, the State Department had been directly involved in forcing his abdication, so one way or another the Government was in line for some scathing criticism on its mishandling of the Iranian situation, however hard THE COMPANY's press and TV outlets might work belatedly to

147

portray the banished monarch as a monster of totalitarian repression.

After all, what really mattered to two hundred million Americans was that some of their garages had started to run dry. How to explain that from now on there might not always be gasoline in the pumps because the Liberal Establishment and the "dirty tricks" brigade of the C.I.A. had so arranged things that a substantial proportion of their oil supplies was dependent on the whim of an elderly mystic who preferred prayer mats to Cadillacs, and the meditative atmosphere of the mosque to the American way of life?

Too late nowadays to lay the blame on the perfidious British, or the French or the Portuguese, who had been convenient whipping boys in earlier crises, — yet whose colonialist forays had at least ensured that vital sources of raw materials remained in friendly and dependable hands! Too late to ask Eisenhower about his policy in the Suez affair of 1956, or Kissinger about the skulduggeries of his shuttle diplomacy! This time it looked as if the President and his advisers were stuck with it themselves.

¶102.   SIGNS OF AN AWAKENING

The band of Iranian "student" revolutionaries who stormed the American Embassy in Teheran in November of 1979, shooting one or two of the Marine defenders and capturing the Embassy staff as hostages, may or may not have been put up to it by THE COMPANY, but they certainly helped to get the Establishment off the hook. Their ransom demands, for a surrender of the Shah and a public investigation of his alleged crimes against the Iranian people, might have seemed eminently negotiable in some quarters, and with American lives at stake, who was to say when the discredited holder of the Peacock Throne would be tossed to the mercy of his accusers? Mohammed Reza Shah was at that time undergoing cancer treatment in a New York hospital, and having already become a victim of political expediency, he could not have relished his chances of survival should the decision be taken to sacrifice him again.

Unexpectedly it did not happen. President Carter, who

until then had conveyed the impression of a myopic groping for his spectacles in a shale bing, was suddenly impelled to stand up and be counted. He warned the Iranian Government that he was concerned about the hostages, and made that somewhat nebulous administration responsible for their safety. But he categorically refused to negotiate the Shah's surrender on any terms, and indeed initiated a series of measures which had potentially far-reaching consequences. These included ordering an American fleet into Iranian waters, and subjecting the Ayatollah's regime to financial sanctions by freezing all its American-held assets.

There were also some peremptory and pre-emptive efforts to involve other Western nations in the financial embargo, but these were treated with understandable caution and some resentment in European capitals. After all, when THE COMPANY and the maverick wing of the C.I.A. put on a show, it's very often the bit part extras and the Johnny-come-latelys who are left to pay for the hall and the outstanding expenses.

But the American public seemed to have no such inhibitions. After thirty-odd years of mildly defeatist propaganda, designed to muffle or muzzle their responses to world events, they suddenly blew their tops on this issue of the Teheran hostages, and gave Carter a loud huzza in his resistance to the attempted blackmail. They also gave vent to their feelings in a domestic context by roughing up Iranian students in the U.S.A. and demanding that they be expelled from their places of education.

Teenagers gave up their pop concerts to demonstrate, and Iranian flags were burned in the streets, — it was all vaguely reminiscent of some of the scenes that had taken place during the period of alienation from the Vietnam War. Then a generation of American youth had cruelly misread the signs as they thoughtlessly condemned their South Vietnamese allies to a Communist future. Now it was some forty or fifty American citizens who had become the innocent pawns of power politics and an Islamic revolution.

Yes, now it was Americans who were being pushed around,

— and Americans were getting mad about it. Could it be that the world crisis was finally making its impact on hometown U.S.A.?

¶103.   THE METEORIC RISE OF JIMMY WHO

The violent seizure of the Teheran Embassy coincided with the beginning of campaigning for the 1980 presidential election, which might be one explanation for Jimmy Carter's sudden conversion to statesmanship. Certainly it is on record that his popularity, which had been at its lowest ebb, perked up dramatically when it was seen that he was not going to bend before Iranian blackmail. What was more, when his Democratic rival Teddy Kennedy endeavoured to capitalise on the situation by making a public criticism of the Shah, the boomerang rebounded upon the whole Kennedy clan, and left the incumbent President as firm favourite for his party's nomination.

Previous to this of course, Carter's record had been little short of catastrophic. He had blundered and bumbled and stuttered his way through three years of executive office till many honest folk began to wonder how he had got there in the first place.

But how *had* he got there? Not by intellect, or administrative experience, or sheer political dynamism! that was for sure. Better, more capable men had fallen by the way. So it had to be some kind of a compromise. The choice, perhaps the negative choice, — of a candidate who would be least offensive to the largest number of people?

Well you're getting warmer. It's something of that nature, but not quite. It is in fact based upon the manner in which Liberal Fabians had so infiltrated both the Democratic and Republican Party machines that they could confidently reckon to block any candidate who threatened to upset their consensus. This was exactly what George Bernard Shaw had in mind when he advised the fledgelings of the newly formed British Fabian Society to go out and permeate all the main political groupings, so that ultimately they would be seen to implement Fabian policies, whichever of the warring factions got themselves elected. Fabianism crossed the Pond in the early days of the twentieth century, and some of Shaw's brilliantly subversive ideas went along with it, so that by the nineteen seventies the disciples of the tortoise and their Establishment backers (that unholy alliance which for convenience we have sometimes called THE COMPANY), had a double lock on the U.S. presidential system that would defy an Olympic wrestler to break it.

Many Americans either knew or suspected this, and having lived through the Vietnam debacle and the phony melodrama of Watergate, were anxiously looking around in search of someone — anyone — who would clean up Washington and confront the oligarchs. So when a Georgian peanut farmer playfully known as Jimmy Who started chalking up impressive victories in the Democratic primaries, naive and well-intentioned souls thought they had found a champion against big power politics and Wall Street's wicked barons. They hoped for a miracle.

Hardened cynics who were well aware of the ingenuity and resources of the Liberal Establishment reckoned that for a country boy to break though, it would take no less than a miracle. Even so, — and despite an abysmal lack of precise information about the principles and capabilities of the Georgian hayseed, — some of them began to feel that they too wanted this miracle, much though their worldly experience had taught them that in this modern age miracles are hard to come by.

But as the Carter bandwaggon continued to roll, there were plenty who felt it would do no harm just to hope and dream. The local man from Plains, Georgia looked as though he was going to make good, — driven onwards and upwards by an electorate which had had enough of slick politicians and the puppets and place men of the Federalist bureaucracy. What did it matter if he stumbled over his speeches, and there was hay growing out of his ears? In the speeches which he did manage to put over, he was telling Americans things they badly wanted to hear. Whatever happened, he said, — whatever his mistakes or his failures, — he would be frank, he would be honest. He would never tell them a lie.

151

Bravo and hosannas! There had been nothing quite like this since Abraham Lincoln came out of his log cabin. So Jimmy Who got the nomination, and went forward to the final round against Gerald Ford, the outgoing president, who was an Establishment man and a member of the CFR. An' darned if good ole Jimmy didn't just walk in there an' scoop the pool! Yessir, the boy from Plains had made it all the way to the presidential chair in the White House. So now we were going to have some good clean homespun politics that hadn't got smutted up with city grime. Finally an outsider had made it, — and the System was breached at last.

¶104. THE POLITICAL COUP OF
THE CENTURY

But *was* he an outsider?

It may have taken a passive and largely brainwashed American electorate more than a couple of years to make up their minds on that point. But some astute Establishment watchers knew the answer even before the new president was ready to name the members of his administration. For a number of the advisers whom he had gathered around him, such as Cyrus Vance, Professor Brzezinski and Michael Blumenthal, were in fact directors of the notorious CFR, that non-elected body set up in 1919 by Fabian Colonel House to monitor and unofficially direct the foreign policy of the United States. Carter himself, as well as Vice-President Mondale, along with Vance, Blumenthal and Brzezinski again, plus Andrew Young, Dr. Harold Brown and various others, were also associated with the Trilateral Commission, which would continue the conspiratorial work of Bilderberg after Prince Bernhardt's exposure and disgrace in 1976. In fact, just about the only well known political adventurer left out of office after Carter had finished his appointments was the jet-shuttling Dr. Henry Kissinger, and *he* had been marooned with the outgoing Ford Administration so as to leave the public with something to vote *against*.

So the Eastern Liberal Establishment, the Fabian oligarchy, the CFR boys of the perpetual hidden government, had pulled it off again, — and in a novel and unpredictable fashion. Jimmy Carter, the peanut farmer from Plains, Georgia, had been their man since 1973. They had groomed him and they had financed him. And when he won the big prize, they were rewarded with a clean sweep of all the important posts in the government.

¶105.   THE STOOGE WHO COULDN'T
         GET SMART ENOUGH

Only one good thing can come out of this horrendous lesson on the depravity of modern American politics. At the very pinnacle of their power, at the pitch of their gloating over the most audacious farce they had ever pulled upon an unsuspecting electorate, the secret oligarchs must have detected one fatal weakness in the grandiose ploy that was surely intended to carry them that much closer to the Collectivist New World Order which had been their long-term objective from the beginning. This stemmed from the small town mediocrity and yawning incompetence of the Georgian hayseed whom they had promoted with skilful press coverage and million dollar campaign funding to the position of President of the United States.

A stooge must be pliant and accommodating. Also, he mustn't be *too* smart. *If* he gets too smart, then he starts to imagine he did it all by himself, — a delusion which apparently afflicted Richard Nixon in his second term of office. Hence the incredible houha of Watergate, — and another salutary lesson of the retribution that awaits those who think they can buck the system.

There seemed little prospect of Jimmy Carter getting too smart. The problem that soon emerged was that he could not get smart at all. It needed a minimum of decorum, intuition and common sense even to go through the motions of being the country's First Executive Officer, and poor bumbling chuckhead Jimmy Who seemed to be lacking in these basic fundamentals.

So the spectacle of a front man who had become a liability and an embarrassment in the mid-term of his presidency was something that was beginning to rub off on the American public, who must obviously have started wondering why, with some

153

two hundred million people at their disposal, — many, many thousands of them possessing high talent, courage, skill and dedication, — the system had to throw up such an inadequate specimen as Plains boy Jimmy Carter. When people start wondering on a subject like that, they also start looking around for reasons. They might even start listening to those patient souls who down through the years had toiled to warn their unsuspecting countrymen of the conspiracy that had them in thrall, — and none of these impending developments was at all favourable to the Fabian oligarchs.

¶106.　　　THE WATERGATE THAT
　　　　　　　　NEVER WAS

So what to do about Jimmy Who? Sit it out? or drive him from office? They had at their disposal an embezzlement and corruption scandal which, even without media exploitation, would have made Watergate look like a harmless practical joke. Bert Lance, a Georgian banker and long time friend and colleague, whom Carter had appointed to a top post in his cabinet as Director of Management and Budget, was forced to resign in September of 1977 when the U.S. Senate started official investigations into irregular and fraudulent practices at his own Calhoun First National Bank. A man called Billy Lee Campbell, a vice president of the Calhoun bank, who in 1976 had been sentenced to eight years imprisonment for his part in the embezzlement of some 900,000 dollars of the bank's resources, later testified that Lance himself had been implicated in the series of false loans which made up the fraudulent appropriation.

The inference was that a considerable proportion of the missing money had gone to finance the banker's abortive campaign for the governorship of Georgia in 1974, — and there were further suspicions and allegations that hometown boy Lance, who had become known as Carter's funding manager in his drive to the presidency, had grossly abused the confidence of his depositors to shuttle and appropriate finance for the presidential campaign as well.

Here was something juicier, potentially more appetising than the crummy little crudities of Watergate. A president of the United States associated with bank frauds and embezzlement! A director of the Management and Budget Office who had to let a former employee take the rap for irregularities which could have implicated him in charges of criminal negligence! Political campaigns that were financed by a mysterious channelling and shuttling of funds from sources that remained totally undisclosed . . . .

Ah! there's the rub. THE COMPANY had enough on Carter to hustle him out of office with much less razzamatazz and synthetic indignation than they had used against Richard Nixon. But the exercise might have been counter-productive, and even dangerous. For if there was any substance to the suspicion that the Carter bandwaggon had been fuelled and victualled by the millionaire monopolists of the CFR and Bilderberg, their most obvious means of implementation was through the local Georgian banks controlled and manipulated by Bert Lance. Just how much of that clandestine operation would be exposed to public scrutiny if they started another Watergate?

¶107.   THE GROOMING OF THE
                    NEXT INCUMBENT

All right! so there was a restricted choice on the matter. For the last year or so of the Carter Administration, conspirators with vast takeover plans in their portfolios would just have to sit on those plans, — and try to be patient.

As from about the middle of 1979 the new darling of the oligarchs was Senator Edward Kennedy, younger brother of the murdered president, and lone survivor of that still unexplained drowning incident at Chappaquiddick. It had been common knowledge that because two of Rose Kennedy's sons died by political assassination, she was reluctant to let her youngest run for high office lest he met a similar fate. But by midsummer 1979, no doubt under considerable pressure, that maternal restriction had finally been lifted, and Edward's hat was in the ring as a challenge to Carter for the 1980 Democratic nomination.

YOUR Exclusive EXPRESS

THE VOICE OF SCOTLAND

SCOTTISH DAILY
EXPRESS

No. 24,631   Thursday September 13 1979   10p

EXPRESS PICTURE BY DEREK HUDSON

Joan Kennedy . . . born to be First Lady

JOAN
Every inch a First Lady

SHE'S glamorous, chic, and exudes the aura and anticipation of someone born to the role of America's first lady.

The only split she's aware of is strictly non-political—it leads straight up the side of her haute couture skirt. And the greatest party division in sight is the deep V-neck of

EXCLUSIVE

her jacket, which parts to reveal a glimpse of bosom.

She is Joan Kennedy, wife of Ted the playboy and womaniser, Ted the senator and powerbroker, and now Ted, the man who could undoubtedly become 40th President of the United States.

Joan has clawed her way back from alcoholism, and a two-year separation from Ted.

Now she is the woman who could bring back to the White House some of the glamour and sophistication of Jackie O.

Read her EXCLUSIVE Interview with Brian Vine on the Centre Pages.

THE GROOMING OF THE NEXT INCUMBENT

That was the signal for a sophisticated press relations campaign to swing into action. Over the ensuing eighteen months a worldwide network of newspapers, magazines and television stations would convey the subtle message that Teddy was the ideal man for the White House in 1981. Ask not how the instructions and the cues would be passed down the line. The author is not privy to the techniques and methods by which the mammoth communications media of the Fabian-Liberal Establishment goes about its devious business. But he does suspect that some of the slicker professionals, given adequate broadcast facilities, could sell ice bricks to Eskimos and air aridifiers to the thirsty denizens of the Kalahari Desert.

The great image-building exercise had quickly been extended to this side of the Pond. For instance in September of 1979 the 'Scottish Daily Express' blossomed forth one morning with a full-length photograph of Mrs. Joan Kennedy, — nobody's pin-up when she was in the throes of a drink problem, and certainly not the most envied of American wives when her playboy husband was treading the primrose path. Now however this Manchester-based Scottish daily was going all out to persuade its wide-eyed readers that the glamorous Joan "exuded the aura and anticipation of someone born to the role of America's first lady".

What a caption! And what confidence! The media boys imagined that they had Teddy well on his way to the White House already. Who cared now about Chappaquiddick, and the life of licence and immorality with which that tragic incident had seemed to be in keeping? The process of building a new image, of promoting a new miracle, had been set in motion. Thenceforth the principal objective of the opinion moulders would be to get across the message that Destiny required another Kennedy. Some of them would be mere professional hacks. Others would take up the refrain because imitation is easier than original thinking. Only an élitist minority would know exactly what they were doing.

They were choosing Kennedy because he was already one of their own kind. Had the senator been available in 1976,

Jimmy Carter would have been not so much a has-been as a never-was. It takes patience and perseverance to run a conspiracy, and the sedulous manipulators who had been trying for years to seduce America into a world federal state devoid of moral values or Christian charity, had been obliged to admit many a rebuff, many a frustration. But every now and then, as with other devious and protracted enterprises, there must have been occasions when they could see a clear way ahead.

This was one such occasion. Kennedy was neither a deep thinker nor a man of principle. He was already known to support many of the liberal-internationalist policies which THE COMPANY would expect him to pursue in office, — and if nasty decisions had to be taken in the drive towards that new world order, nasty controversial decisions which the nation bitterly resented and regretted, there would also be the aura and the magic of the family name to help him and them sell the package to a suspicious electorate.

In the domestic and international circumstances that were looming towards the end of Jimmy Carter's first term in the presidency, Americans would need the big spending world federalist Edward Kennedy like they would need the proverbial hole in the head. But it was becoming more and more certain that in the days of their decision-making, their Rockefeller-sponsored daily newspaper and their local television station would be eloquently persuading them that holes in the head, — and Teddymania — were coming right into fashion.

The *lemmus Americanus* is by no means the least numerous of the species. It abounds in many of the sub-groupings we have noted in the United Kingdom. And as illustrated by that quaint offering from the *'Scottish Daily Express'* on Joan Kennedy's proclivities as a future First Lady, it keeps in touch with its cousins on this side of the Atlantic. There are not too many votes to be won for Teddy in Auchenshuggle or Drumnadrochit, but you have to hand it to THE COMPANY's press relations corps for getting in there early, and endeavouring to cover all the angles.

Normally in a study such as this, we are conducting a series of post-mortems, — tracing what happened in the recent or more distant past, and endeavouring to explain why it happened. But in the affair of Jimmy Carter and his successor-designate for the presidential contest of 1980, we were privileged to get right in on the action, with hopes of anticipating some of the moves in the great new power game that was just beginning.

¶108. WRONG ABOUT THE ANGLO-SAXONS?

All that was, of course, before the events in Iran and neighbouring Afghanistan gave a lame-duck president a *raison d'être*, and a chance to strike a sympathetic accord with an electorate which still, at heart, wanted its elected leader to speak and act decisively as spokesman for a great and powerful nation. Such was the significance of Carter's quick surge in popularity in response to Iranian blackmail over the siege at the Teheran Embassy. Such also was the general approval for his reactions to Russia's Afghan adventure. Electioneering assumes a diminished role when a country's security is threatened, — and it is true to say that at this very late hour the Americans had finally felt themselves to be threatened.

The invasion of Afghanistan could scarcely be regarded as a COMPANY ploy. It was not in their inimitable style, and had nothing to commend it as a step towards the new One World Order, — which was to come about as the West drooled and drivelled itself into collectivist bondage, not as the result of an act of flagrant aggression which would set the pulses racing and the adrenalin flowing.

This is not to say that the Marxist-Fabian Establishment had no responsibility for the cruel fate that befell the Afghan nation during the winter snows of 1979-80. The part they had played over the years was in equipping the Muscovite comrades with lots of expensive technology and destructive toys, which the latter were eventually tempted into using. By their influence upon events and policy, they had also encouraged a belief that the Western peoples were already too far gone in decadence and self-indulgence to retrieve their lost leadership.

But that could be a miscalculation. The Anglo-Saxon and

159

Celtic races who would be called upon to restore the military and technological power balance were not yet degenerate and impotent, — merely bemused and drugged into a torpor of self-abasement, from which they could still be roused by a shock awakening.

In the United States at the end of 1979 there were a few signs of just such an awakening. At least some of the lemming folk had guessed what lay ahead, and were turning back before they reached the edge of the precipice.

CHAPTER FOURTEEN

Britain and the Advent of
¶109.   Margaret Thatcher

What now of our own country, — and with particular
reference to the events of May 3rd 1979, when we were reckoned
to have put the first genuine conservative into Downing Street
since the days of Winston Churchill? How does that claim
measure up against the truly horrific disclosures which we have
felt obliged to make about the state of American politics? Will
it emerge that some of our own cherished political dogmas are
as phony and synthetic as some that have been exposed over
there? And will we find, to our dismay and disappointment,
that the new Prime Minister Mrs. Thatcher is the stooge and
hostage of some powerful internationalist cartel linked with
Wall Street and the CFR?

We hope not. The author himself believes that Margaret
Thatcher could be the best thing that has happened to British
and European politics for a very long time. But this will not be
so if her natural supporters stand back in uncritical admiration,
and allow her to be pressurised by the many entrenched influences which oppose her reactive policies, and are bent on
neutralising them. Some of this opposition comes from within
her own party, where it should be exposed and highlighted on
every possible occasion, so that there can be no false assessment
of her strengths and weaknesses. But there are also external
factors, an account of which may usefully fill the ensuing
pages of this chapter.

A LADY OF INDEPENDENT
¶110. MIND?

In the recent past the British Conservative Party has suffered almost as much from the politics of the consensus as its Labour and Liberal rivals. When George Bernard Shaw handed out that epic injunction to his youthful disciples before the turn of the century, he did not mean that they should stop short of the Primrose League or the doors of the Carlton Club. Like an old Indian fighter, he obviously relished the idea of downing his opponents from the least expected quarter. So the Tories got their Fabian influx, not from the lower orders, but from their snobbiest schools and universities, and from a limp and cringing aristocracy which seemed to assume that its best contribution to twentieth century progress was to cast aside both its privileges and its responsibilities, and thus disenburdened, show everyone else a clean pair of heels in the retreat from reality.

Mrs. Thatcher was a grocer's daughter from Grantham. She was therefore able to grow up without guilt complexes or any of the sillier examples of inverted thinking which had come into vogue through belated upper class absorption of the Fabian ethic. She was also the type of person who would be permanently condemned to minor office in an era of consensus politics, so when Edward Heath's leadership was challenged after his second election defeat of October 1974, the fact that Mrs. T.'s floral bonnet went into the ring along with the trilbys and deerstalkers of her masculine opponents scarcely caused a flutter in the power centres of Europe and America. Ladbroke's made her a long odds outsider for a contest in which the federalist-minded Heath was expected to reassert his disputed authority.

We know now that things did not happen that way. It was an intriguing election from the viewpoint of those who had learned from long experience that candidates for high office seldom get through the preliminaries without being cornered by pressure groups, and having to dilute their policies and their principles with exasperating compromises. Margaret Thatcher

162

did not *seem* to indulge in any such manoeuvrings. Hers looked to be an independent candidature. Prior to the initiation of the election procedure, she had not even been considered as a potential starter, so there would be little opportunity for outside elements to sound out her views, make bargains, offer hidden inducements, or otherwise attempt to influence her towards their own way of thinking. Here, perchance, was one instance where the Fabian technique of cultivating all factions and viewpoints had gone by default. A leader had come through to take charge of a major political party without a smear or a hint of compromise or consensus, – or of being beholden to anyone except the British electorate for a fulfilment of the promises that she would make in her bid to gain political power.

¶111.   INVITATION TO BILDERBERG

But if they had ignored her previous to her dramatic victory, they soon remedied that oversight. Thatcher's change in status was recognised almost immediately, when she was invited to the 1975 Bilderberg Conference, held that year at Cesme, a remote spot on the Aegean Coast of Turkey. That she accepted was recorded by an alert if unofficial photographer, who snapped her in an apparently amiable chit-chat with Robert S. MacNamara, President of the World Bank, and a man close to the centre of the Bilderberg Conspiracy.

What Margaret Thatcher thought and saw and said during those three days at Cesme are very much her own business, – and she was probably not inclined to talk about it. She was one of only several British representatives, another being Denis Healey, one time Communist, at that time Chancellor of the Exchequer, – and long-time member of the British Fabian Society. Whether she realised it or not, she was also in the presence of dedicated One Worlders, men of great wealth and power for whom the concept of a World Federalist State had become an all-devouring obsession, – and who were willing cold-bloodedly to contemplate riot, assassination, famine, revolution and terrorism as legitimate means for furthering their schemes of global hegemony. Here were gathered the paymasters for

163

subversion in Southern Africa, for guerrilla wars in corners of
South America, and for the continuing carnage in Northern
Ireland, — though needless to say, such sensitive issues would
not be discussed in open session.

We do not know whether Mrs. Thatcher was invited to
Cesme to observe, to receive instructions, or to be duly impressed
and overawed by the fantastic power and prestige of this élitist
supra-national organisation which could persuade the Turkish
Government to give it more privacy and security than a meeting
of the heads of sovereign states. What we do know is that when
the next Bilderberg conference came round she was busily
engaged elsewhere, — which was a wise decision for a lady who
aspired to become Prime Minister of Great Britain. For as C.
Gordon Tether observed in his Lombard column of the Financial
Times, May 6, 1975, — a column which he was subsequently
banned from writing, — the people of Great Britain were entitled
to expect more of their elected leaders than that they should
engage in secret conferences in obscure corners of the world
with sinister international figures who were accountable to no
one.

SEARCHING FOR HIDDEN
¶112. PRESSURES

So when the Conservatives duly won the General Election
of May 1979, it was not necessarily a time for all good patriots
to breathe a heartfelt sigh of thankfulness, put their feet up,
and proceed once more to leave everything to the professionals.
True that the policies successfully promoted had the stamp of a
leader who believed in what she was doing, who had promised
to take government out of the people's lives, and to restore
their freedom of choice in large sectors of the national life. What
was more, — what was historic and virtually unprecedented since
the advent of the Fabian consensus, — she had committed herself
to a *reversal* of the socialist progression, a winding back and a
positive retrenchment, rather than a passive if reluctant acceptance of revolutionary trends, as Heath and MacMillan had done
before her. Yes Thatcher seemed every inch a conservative, —

and moreover a personality with the charm, determination and innate conviction that could see her policies through to fruition.

Was it fair therefore, in her hour of victory, to recall that one occasion four years previously, when she had hobnobbed with a bunch of well-heeled internationalist wreckers whose aims and beliefs were so diametrically opposed to her own? For no one, even in irrelevant levity, could ever accuse the Bilderbergers of being conservatives. The whole guiding purpose of their clandestine movement had been towards a monoply of power, based on great wealth, on cartelist intrigue, and on that pressurising of peoples and governments which can only come through a gradual but remorseless advance of collectivism. Strange company for the grocer's daughter from Grantham, who had promised to free the British nation from the strangling bonds which the Bilderbergers and their Fabian collaborators had wrapped so tightly round them!

Yet Prince Bernhardt and his secretariat must have known all these things before they invited her along. So why did they persist? Was it because they wanted to meet her at close quarters, to size her up, plumb her ideological attachments, figure out some way in which she could be *used* to their own advantage?

¶113. INFILTRATION FROM THE RIGHT

Suffice it to say that they would not be put off by her sheer conservatism. For THE COMPANY had used conservatives before.

Take the case of Richard Nixon, who rose to fame for his determined pursuit and exposure of the notorious Alger Hiss. That stamped the then youthful congressman as a patriot and anti-Communist, an impression that was enhanced in the minds of the American public by his support of Senator McCarthy when the latter was conducting his campaign to get spies and subversives out of the U.S. administration. Yet Nixon had already turned left when he accepted the Vice-presidency under Eisenhower. His ambitions and his impatience to get to the top had induced him to accept the patronage of the Liberal-Fabian clique who even then were assuming a dominant position in

165

American politics. But he did not signal his change of heart and principles, as an honest man might do, by resigning from the Republican Party, which had traditionally represented the conservative point of view. Had he done so, he would promptly have outlived his usefulness, and ceased to enjoy that patronage which was his passport to fame and fortune.

So he did exactly what was required of him, stayed plumb in the heart of the Republican movement, campaigned tirelessly for its candidates of whatever political conviction, and all the time moved his party further to the liberal left, so that in 1960 the *Wall Street Journal* was obliged to remark of the coming presidential contest that Nixon's brand of Liberal Republicanism had brought him so close to his Democrat opponent that the American electorate was being denied a *freedom of choice.*

Where have we heard that one before? The Fabian oligarchy had got their consensus, — and they had achieved it through a devious politician who was first introduced to the public as an *ultra* and an anti-communist.

¶114. POWERS OF REWARD AND RETRIBUTION

So where does that leave us in this strange episode of Mrs. Thatcher and the Bilderbergers? It would be naive to make direct comparisons between the lean and hungry Nixon of the 1960's and the successful lady who in May of 1979 had made it to Downing Street entirely on her own merits. Unlike Tricky Dick, who got to rely upon Fabian help, *she* had got to the top in spite of them. Also, if it was a matter of bribes and blandishments now that she had gained power, there did not seem such a great deal that they could offer her. Ridiculous to talk in terms of money or prestige! The lady had wealth and position of her own, and would not be interested. Some softening of the Fabian-socialist opposition within the United Kingdom? Perhaps a disastrous fragmentation of the Labour Party through the elevation of Wegwood Benn! A reduction of its electoral appeal so that it became a laughing stock! Margaret Thatcher as the longest reigning prime minister since Walpole! This is something which those Big, Big People at Bilderberg, through their fantastic wealth and influence, might conceivably be able to deliver.

And if the carrot failed, what about the stick? For we shall have laboured in vain if by this time we have not achieved a modicum of credibility for our contention that THE COMPANY can be both a distributor of largesse and a scourge to those who get in its way. A high-principled reactionary operating from Downing Street would be very much in its way, — in fact the equivalent of a blockage on the freeway, — and they must try either to move her or to *use* her, — use her as they used Richard Nixon, so that her very conservatism might be put up as a screen behind which COMPANY policies could be pursued with a minimum of hindrance.

If we cannot be made to believe, you and I, that Margaret Thatcher would ever consent to becoming such a stooge, then we must be ready for, and informed about, the other alternative, — the situation where a Machiavellian conspiratorial network sets about taking her political career apart.

After all, she came to power at a time when those self-same conspiratorial forces were deliberately turning our world upside down. We were beset with debilitating industrial sabotage at home; a terrorist war across the Irish Sea; looming threats to our lifelines and sources of essential raw materials; persistent subversive campaigns against every state and organisation which might help us to guard those lifelines and secure the strategic supplies; revolutions popping up in the most critical places, all apparently unexpected and at the least opportune moments.

It would not be protocol in official quarters to mention that these recurring disasters might just be connected, part of an overall plan. Yet evidence was there a-plenty to show that the connections existed, — some of them having been exposed in this volume. We shall not have started to turn back the collectivist tide till we begin talking frankly and openly about problems of national survival, and the real reasons why thus far these problems have seemed so intractable, and incapable of solution. If you don't recognise an enemy in the bloke who's lunging at

**MARGARET THATCHER with
ROBERT MACNAMARA
at Bilderberg.**

DAVID ROCKEFELLER

your jugular vein, how in God's name can you ward off the deadly blow, — and take the necessary steps to ensure there will be no recurrence?

¶115.   CUTTING BACK STATE
                         INTERVENTION

Margaret Thatcher has always been fair game for the trade union leader, the Labour politician and the bureaucrat intent upon an ever proliferating bureaucracy. To them her ideal of making all services and all industries cost accountable, — and accountable in so far as is possible to the exacting standards of the market economy, — is a form of heresy which in a less inhibited age would have seen her burned at the stake. Those whose unsubsidised economic activites have always had to be conducted on that rational basis, — the housewife who shops within her income, the worker who claims his whack in pay and bonuses from a profit-making enterprise, the manufacturer who has to keep his quality, his costs and his selling prices within a range which the market will accept and absorb, have all been accustomed to operating within a monetary discipline which applies its own automatic regulators, and functions without the intervention of governments. There is nothing ideological about monitoring the shopping budget, *earning* a fat wage packet or promoting one's goods and services in the market place.

The intervention of the state into all forms of entre- preneurial activities is on the other hand extremely ideological, and where it involves, — as inevitably happens, — the subsidi- sation of one worker's efforts by a levy upon the productivity of another, there is relevance in a mass of co-related factors, such as the social desirability of the subsidised activity, the willingness of the productive worker to go on accepting a lower living standard so that the subsidy can continue, and the efficacy with which the state assisted service or industry responds to the challenge of becoming a charge upon the national exchequer.

In this last respect the record is almost universally bad. Throughout the last thirty years, during which the British economy has been ideologically slanted towards a higher and higher degree of state intervention, it has been established beyond reasonable doubt that wherever a group, a service or an industrial sector has been relieved of the discipline of market viability, its costs and its productivity have promptly hiked off in different directions until one quickly lost sight of the other. Up to the early nineteen-sixties, for instance, Britain had a clutch of progressive and prosperous steel companies whose predecessors had jointly inspired and fostered the industrial revolution. The sum of their profitability was a considerable benefit to the national budget, in that they annually paid over an appreciable slice of their surpluses to the Inland Revenue for the defraying of government expenditures elsewhere.

¶116. THE DISASTER OF NATIONALISED STEEL

Following Harold Wilson's election victory in 1964, and for no other reason than satisfying the Fabian urge to control all means of *production, distribution and exchange*, those healthy and progressive steel companies were amalgamated into a mammoth nationalised corporation which, when Margaret Thatcher got to Downing Street, was reckoned to be losing about one million pounds a day. In the interim period, through having its forward planning programmed by an unaccountable bureaucracy, and having additionally been favoured by the injection of mind-boggling sums of taxpayers' money, it had created a steel-making capacity which was subsequently discovered to be grossly in excess of requirements, − all at a cost which, in spite of the massive annual subsidies, had made its products so uncompetitive that its domestic market, once the jealously nurtured preserve of the private steelmakers, was being eroded by price-conscious overseas rivals.

Meanwhile, labour-wise, the old economic observances about manning and viability had apparently been jettisoned. Where the state-capitalisation programme had taken a realistic jump into the future by the installation of new sophisticated technology, its beneficial effects were promptly neutralised by protracted trade union wrangles which no cost-conscious privately owned enterprise would willingly have suffered for more than twenty-four hours. And in the Clyde Estuary a multi-million pound iron ore terminal, built for economic loading of Scotland's most advanced steelworks at Ravenscraig, was allowed to lie idle for a costly and exasperating six months as dockers and steel unions argued over who would be responsible for what. Millions and millions of taxpayer-contributed funds squandered in meaningless meandering! Foreign competitors prompted and even encouraged to take a share of our markets, — aye, virtually to take over the British worker's job and leave him as an industrial backnumber!

¶117.   THE COMPANY AS A SUBTLE
AND INSIDIOUS ENEMY

It was this process of debilitating state protectionism which Margaret Thatcher had promised to reverse, and for which a majority of the electorate had given her a prospective five-year tenancy of 10 Downing Street. In the first flush of enthusiasm many of her new-found supporters, having just come off a prolonged trip into Fabian statism, had not considered that some of the withdrawal symptoms were likely to be painful. And her ideological opponents in the socialist hierarchy, who knew perfectly well that many of their entrenched powers and bureaucratic empires were scheduled to disappear even if she were only partially successful, had already resolved to fight her bitterly and uncompromisingly along every inch of the way.

Add to this the essentially destructive and demoralising activities of THE COMPANY, that unholy consortium of Big Bankers and way out revolutionaries with its pressure points on both sides of the ideological divide. It has already been clearly indicated that their overweening ambitions must lead them to favour a state collectivist political structure, since only by such means could the Fabian-monopolists ensure perpetuation of their illegitimate power. Thus COMPANY policy is bound to oppose Thatcher in those areas where she is seen to be diminishing government and widening individual rights and responsibilities. The loyal COMPANY man will deprecate, denigrate and patronisingly remonstrate whenever he senses that an element of the counter philosophy has been reduced to stalemate by combined opposition. Already he is trying to anticipate the day when Thatcherism collapses, and when, presumably, the process of creeping collectivisation can be continued where it left off.

¶118.　　THE CONSENSUS AND THE
SOVIET THREAT

And what about the rest of us, as with strikes, industrial sabotage and bitter unreasoning opposition, the Thatcher Government is seen to be having a very stormy passage? Since we can't all be card-carrying members of the Tory Party, do we stand back with a smug sense of detachment, and the complacent assumption that whatever happens, we don't really need to be implicated? After all, who's to say that things would not be going more smoothly under Edward Heath, or Big Jim Callaghan or David Steel, — or perhaps a cosy coalition of all three together? The ideal consensus solution! National unity and all that! Everybody putting his best foot forward with a firm hand, a touch on the tiller, and a little of what you fancy does you good! None of this abrasive stuff about winding back the ratchet, containing the bureaucracy and restoring commercial viability to public sector industries!

Well of course, in the aftermath of the Russian invasion of Afghanistan, even the most purblind little lemming may just possibly agree that there are two distinct aspects of good national government, the internal and the external, the domestic and the image that is projected abroad. In this latter respect, nothing matters as much and as urgently as the front that we present to Soviet imperialism, for many years thought to have been comfortably contained by détente and arms limitation talks and spheres of hegemony.

So who has the nerve and the proper instincts for dealing with that ever-present threat to our security and national survival? Where amongst the demoralised and discredited protagonists of our corrupt and degenerating code of Western values is there a philosophy and a set of principles which will inoculate us against the spreading collectivist disease; which will secure and strengthen us against the gathering storm?

¶119. FORMING A PROTECTIVE BARRIER

On a pouring wet night, for instance, if you've been unlucky enough to get a fireball through the roof, how do you set about sealing off the break and minimising the damage? Do you strip the bed and stuff the hole with a blanket, — or pack it with foam insulation? Or do you remember that in the toolshed you've got a zinc plate or a square of sheet steel? In any case you'll be scrambling for some material which will act as a *barrier* to the continuing downpour, rather than a palliative which will quickly become sodden and drip through when it's saturated.

Let's try again! They're fond of talking about *barrier* treatments in paint technology, where the problem is one of bleeding and contamination. Ask a paint chemist how to stop black spots coming through on your white-painted wall, or the new emulsion rubbing up the old distemper on the attic bedroom, which hasn't been decorated since grandma was a girl. He'll come up with some kind of sealer, formulated with a special resin which remains impervious to black spots, emulsion and distemper alike. He'll have provided a barrier, on top of which you can happily experiment with your fresh colour schemes whilst the contaminated and friable surfaces lie inert beneath.

¶120. DAVID STEEL AND THE LIBERAL REVIVAL

O.k. So where do *we* get such a barrier, when we're beset with conflagration, contamination, penetration, — and rainwater pouring through on to the keys of the grand piano? Big Jim — or his likely successor? Well actually, that would be the blanket remedy. Maybe a big thick woollen blanket, — but a blanket just the same, liable to get sodden and saturated as the absorbent fibres soak up the precipitation and let it filter through to the erstwhile sheltered areas within.

Then what about the Boy David, father of the first abortion bill, inspirational genius of the Lib-Lab Pact of 1976-78, and shining knight in gleaming armour to about six million *lemmi moderati* who fondly imagine him to be the spiritual successor of Gladstone and Lloyd George? It is perhaps difficult, if not impossible, to persuade these immutable disciples of the middle way that trendy liberalism can be more of a whirlpool than a safe haven when it's the tide of Marxist collectivism that's in flood, — that far from being a barrier, it is more like a catalyst which blends and fuses all the discordant and subversive elements together, — that 'the *avant-garde* of all revolutions, all social cataclysms, all disintegration of ordered societies into repression and tyranny, has been a nebulous liberal intelligentsia, all gas and no substance, which erodes the sturdy certainties in a nation's prideful being, substituting doubt and the paralysis of self-effacement.

We've had it all down through the years, haven't we? We know all the symptoms, so let's be darned sure that we don't lose sight of the basic disease. As for the prospective Liberal revival, — and that young Mr. Steel to seal off the hole in the roof, — despite the metallurgical ring about his name, he would be just about as wet and effective as a squelchy sponge.

¶121.
THE REVOLUTIONARY PHILOSOPHIES ARE NO PROTECTION

All right! We've had our fun with the soppy sponges and the wet blankets, — and the rainwater just keeps dripping through. You always knew the right answer, — at least to the practical problem of roof repair. But when it comes to political theories and ideologies, fallacies and absurdities are not always so clearly highlighted.

The fact is that Fabianism, liberalism and democratic socialism, because they all embody a revolutionary element within their social doctrine, cannot insulate and preserve us against the collectivist metamorphosis. Had Marx-Stalinism been libertarian and benevolent, as many of its early disciples must sincerely have imagined it to be, the socialist and gradualist

174

tendencies within our society would have been the fusing and ameliorating influences, dissolving out the suspicions and the discordancies as we came to be absorbed into a milieu which was accepted for the common good.

But that is not the hypothesis which confronts the Western World today. It is established beyond any doubt that the great majority of us do not wish to be absorbed, — that we have looked the collectivist monster in the maw, and are filled with revulsion and horror.

THE NEED TO UNDERSTAND
¶122.　　　THATCHER CONSERVATISM

So it's back to the barrier, — the set of principles that will seal us off against contamination and infiltration, that will provide us with a resolve and a counter-philosophy upon which to build our national resurgence. In practical terms, ruling out minority creeds and privately held beliefs which have no universal hope of acceptance, — as we stand upon the threshold of the eighties, — the only major political force which can provide us with that insulation, that decontamination barrier, is Thatcher-style conservatism, a unique product of a System which seemed to guard against any possibility of such a remarkable emergence.

The main need for all of us at this stage is to understand these matters, to appreciate the areas where high principle, patriotism and single-mindedness make Margaret Thatcher such a precious national asset, — but at the same time to seek out those contradictory aspects where her philosophy, or that of her chosen team, seems less than watertight against the seepage of collectivist Fabiana which may have been around with us so long that its potency as a dilutant and a contaminant has been dangerously under-estimated.

It is within the permanent state bureaucracy that much of this corrosive medium is lying about, often unattended or without adequate safety precautions, and some newly fledged Tory ministers, coming into contact, regrettably appear to have shown as much resistance to the contagious permeant as would a piece of blotting paper.

One or two such instances are reported in the pages that follow.

CHAPTER FIFTEEN

¶123. Facets of the New Morality

It is possible to be relatively light-hearted about those occasions where members of the new Tory hierarchy fall prey to "the new morality". Mr. Hector Munro, Mrs. Thatcher's appointment at the Ministry of Sport, provided an early illustration of this when he became implicated in the sort of orchestrated hou-ha which erupts every time one or other of the home rugby unions decides to have an exchange of visits with the South Africans.

In recent years rugby has emerged as one of the very few organised recreations to keep its eye on the ball and its mind on the game, in an era when almost every other on-field or off-field activity has been smitten with political overtones. In a madhouse, the deranged and irrational inmates may occasionally descend in fury upon any corner of their frantic domain where a modicum of sanity still persists, and so it was to prove with the muddied oafs of the oval ball, who just kept on doing their own thing, mindless of the storms that broke around them.

Mr. Munro got his initiation into sportopolitics when the Barbarians, a multiracial South African club side, were invited to play a series of matches in the home countries during the autumn of 1979. It was not intended to be a prestige visit. The Barbarians had no pretensions to rival the quality or the crowd-pulling power of the mighty Springboks, but that made little difference to those who had already embraced the Marxist-

177

Fabian concept of sport as an expression of ideological commitment, and who saw in the continued isolation of South African sportsmen an instrument of revolutionary change.

It appeared that a Commonwealth Games committee, meeting at peaceful Gleneagles in the heartland of Scotland, had ruled against all sporting links with the Boer Republic, that the Tories, somewhere in their shadier past, had ratified that commitment, and that the new boy at Minisport had got caught up in something which was not of his own making. So he was expected to put pressure on those mavericks of the rugby scene, for fear that the disgusting exercise of their rights as free men should jeopardise our relationships with the Commonwealth *et alia* in all those other track and field events where organisers and competitors alike had meekly toed the politicised Marxist line.

Mr. Peter Hain, the South African renegade and anti-apartheid campaigner who had achieved fame, if not fortune, when he managed to stop the cricket test series of 1970, was to the fore again with a threat that rugby union intransigence might be used to provoke the Afro-Asian nations into proposing a boycott of the British athletic teams for the Moscow Olympics of 1980.

That really got the sporting lemmings in a tizzy. How the professional track watchers sweated on the possible loss of their free tickets to that sportopolitical jamboree which could conceivably develop into the same kind of totalitarian propaganda exercise that had repelled and disgusted the Western democracies during Hitler's Berlin Olympics of 1936! Forty-four years further on the morality had changed, and those tough guys with the stop watches and the running track vocabulary were unlikely to lose any sleep over the wretches of the Gulag Archipelago. But they were ready to commit mayhem on the naive and selfish clots who were willing to fly in the face of all the principles of *sportopolitik* just to play a few representative games of rugby.

So what did the new Minister of Sport do and say about all this? It was after all a splendid opportunity for him to put the whole sporting fraternity right on the double standards and the hypocrisies of the new morality, — to emphasise as of yore that the traditional British interest in sport was concerned with its relevance to body and character building, — that by time-honoured custom it was the game that was the thing, and the playing of it more important than the winning.

¶124.   FEARS OF AN OLYMPIC
                        BOYCOTT

What did he do? Just what did he do? Did he tell any of those sporting lemmings, those politicised creeps, that they had forgotten the first principles of the activity they were supposed to be reporting, — that they were being made the dupes and the pliant collaborators in a philosophy that would fain destroy us all? Not him! Not so far as we can discover! He got worried stiff at the prospect that the Olympian administrators of the International Sports Committee might just be persuaded to ban the British contingent from the propaganda spectacle in Moscow. So he went to work on his erstwhile colleagues in the rugby unions, and exerted what pressures were available to him in an effort to have the South African tour invitation withdrawn. Fortunately he had not been vested with the power to *order* a withdrawal, otherwise there is no doubt that the rugby control bodies would have faced a Government ban similar to that which stopped a Springbok tour of France. But he did publicise the fact that he considered the Barbarians visit to be "inadvisable", — and that way he kept the Springboks in the official doghouse, whilst maintaining his *rapport* with the exponents of *sportopolitik*. He also must have found himself moseying about amongst the lemming folk, — and wondered how he got there.

¶125.   A CASE OF DISGUSTING
                        HYPOCRISY

Soon, of course, it was all to be swept into the limbo by the Russian invasion of Afghanistan during the New Year of 1980. Then it was the erstwhile sane and sensible citizens of this nation who were calling for boycotts as it was realised how the Soviets could legitimise their aggression if they were allowed to host the peaceful and symbolic Olympic ceremony just a few months afterwards. Both the American and British governments got themselves involved. President Carter wanted to withdraw the U.S. athletic contingent entirely. Mrs. Thatcher proposed switching the Games to the old 1976 venue at Montreal. America's Olympic representatives, at their first reaction, seemed to be indicating that if the President wanted them to stay away from Moscow, they would comply with his wishes. But the clutch of lemming folk who did the talking for Britain's athletic associations, — and who had already shown their taste for *sportopolitik*, — declared that they would be going to Russia regardless. And the International Olympic Sports Committee, which had tolerated many a piece of political blackmail in its postwar history, — which in particular had meekly submitted to a disgraceful Afro-Asian ultimatum against the Rhodesian multi-racial Olympic team in 1972, — whose equivocal attitude on South African rugby tours had so recently caused a British minister to fear an Olympic boycott, — merely stated vis-à-vis the new situation with the Soviet Union, *that it did not wish to mix politics with sport.*

Well! well! And who said there wasn't such a thing as "selective indignation"? Mr. Hector Munro must have been more confused than ever.

¶126.   FLUORIDATION — THE ISSUE
            OF ENFORCED MEDICATION

Now! another instance where some of Mrs. Thatcher's chosen team seem to be failing in their brief to carry out the counter-collectivist principles of their spirited and resolute leader! Anyone not heard of fluoridation, — the proposal to put a compound of fluorine into the public water supply, ostensibly as a means of reducing dental decay? This is essentially a collectivist ploy, since it would have to be imposed against the wishes of perhaps a majority of the country's adult citizens, who would resent being subjected to a mass form of medication.

Indeed, wherever enforced medication has been adopted as an act of policy, it has been condemned as totalitarianism, and resisted by free men to the extent of their capability. One of the worst of Hitler's war crimes was when he submitted the inmates of his concentration camps to experimental surgery and the forcible administering of drugs and medicines with previously unknown effects. Likewise, a beastly and much reviled aspect of the Soviet medical system is its callous and immoral use of sedatives, mind drugs, stimulants and depressives to break the resistance of dissident elements, — a process which in extreme form, can reduce the subject to a human vegetable.

CONTRACEPTION VIA THE
¶127.　　　　WATER SUPPLY

In the United States, where the Soviet system has a surprising number of medical admirers, physicists and psychiatrists obsessed with the need for some form of population control, have already gone on record as suggesting that drugs should be compulsorily administered to inhibit the human reproductive cycle; and spelling it out more clearly, a biologist called Paul Ehrlich is quoted as saying that they might ultimately have to "institute a system whereby a temporary sterilant would be added to a staple food *or to the water supply*", presumably with antidotes sold on licence to those who were allowed to have a family.

With such nightmarish suggestions already on the lips of "experts", any tampering with our water supplies is obviously a matter of public concern. In past years water authorities have been subject to strict regulation and supervision, all for the purpose of ensuring a pure and potable product when the ordinary citizen turns on his tap. If a government ever established the right to put a medical substance into our domestic water, once the principle had been conceded, was there any guarantee that it would stop there? and even if it did, just how awkward and difficult would it be for the nonconforming individual to escape the medication which the state said was good for him? Also, how did all this measure up with freedom of choice and individual liberties?

¶128. THE CANCER-LINK CONTROVERSY

Apart from the ethical aspect, fluoridation was by now a highly contentious scientific and medical issue. The point of fiercest controversy involved the cancer-link statistics which had been produced by American bio-chemists Dean Burk and John Yiamouyiannis, as a result of a twenty year survey over ten fluoridated cities, matched for population and environmental features with ten similar cities which had remained unfluoridated. The statistical graph of cancer deaths over the whole period, and for all the populations surveyed, showed a rising incidence in the fluoridated cities of about forty persons per hundred thousand people. These figures were quickly challenged by the National Cancer Institute in America and the Royal College of Physicians in the United Kingdom, which both produced amended data purporting to refute the Burk-Yiamouyiannis findings, but at a subsequent court hearing in Pittsburg, Pennsylvania, where the whole subject was explored in exhaustive detail under testimony from acknowledged experts on both sides, it was admitted under oath that there had been collusion between the N.C.I. and their counterparts from the Royal College, that this had also involved a Fellow of the Royal Statistical Society, that they had all been working from the same set of erroneously compiled material, — and that, when the errors were removed, the Burk-Yiamouyiannis study did indeed point to a subsequent rise in cancer deaths where water supplies had been fluoridated.

¶129. THE DREADFUL PRECEDENT OF THALIDOMIDE

Cancer deaths! Moral issues! Furious technical arguments about the interpretation of statistics! Accusations of cover-up tactics, rigging of health boards, total obliteration of data unfavourable to the fluoridationist cause! A learned doctor of the Royal College of Physicians forced to admit under oath that he had falsely published as original research in England erroneous figures compiled by the N.C.I. in America! A member of the Royal Statistical Society confessing that he also had used the same erroneous material, and issued it as an independent survey! Writs and counter writs! Eminent figures in the scientific and medical professions of the United States and Europe standing toe to toe, and conducting a verbal punch-up with no holds barred and no quarter given!

Was there ever a better reason for calling a moratorium on the whole business until tempers had cooled, and patient research had had time to consider and impartially evaluate the conflicting claims and arguments? The Province of Quebec had done just that in August of 1977, and two years later had still apparently learned nothing that would encourage it to start fluoridating again. Amongst our partners in the European Community, France and Germany have strict laws against the adulteration of food and drink, — and that includes fluoride, — the Dutch Parliament voted it right out of Holland after debating the Burk-Yiamouyiannis cancer-link statistics, and Belgium, Italy and Austria do not appear to have given the matter any great consideration. But up in Scandinavia, where it was considered very seriously indeed, the Swedes threw it out eventually because they could not get satisfactory assurances on the health risks.

Significant point, eh? Remember thalidomide! Significant enough to the Swedes and the Germans, French and the Dutch, — but not to the backroom boys at the British Ministry of Health. A decade earlier, when Richard Crossman was their chief, he had told them to *fluoridate and be damned*, and they were still conspiring busily to comply with that instruction, regardless of what had come to light in the years between.

So how was the Thatcher Government going to handle this contentious situation, — which in the circumstances it could well do without? Would it stand upon the principles of its dynamic leader, and defend the public's right not to imbibe a chemical it did not want? Or pressurised by the bureaucrats of the Health Department, would it succumb to the new morality and legislate for fluoride by tap water? In October of 1979 a report by the Sunday Observer suggested rather ominously that the latter course was being favoured, since the Government were then said to be "preparing legislation" that would make fluoridation compulsory. However, when the honest-to-goodness journalist who had written the article checked with his sources of information, there was a rapid retreat from the implication of governmental involvement. It appeared that it was merely the Department of Health playing games, — flying kites, testing the temperature, sounding out the opposition, generally skirmishing around the defences to see whether anyone had left a gate unattended or a drawbridge lowered.

MR. FAIRGRIEVE DOES AN ABOUT TURN
¶130.

One might think that at this stage the "freedom of choice" devotees in the Tory hierarchy would start to look warily at this presumptuous civil service bureaucracy which seemed intent upon pursuing its own fixations and obsessions regardless of the policies and principles of the elected government. But there is at least one thoroughly authenticated story which should alert a trusting citizenry against putting too much faith in parties and party politicians, whatever their creed or complexion.

The National Anti-Fluoridation Campaign, run by a formidable chip off Old Britannia called P. Clavell Blount, had for some years kept a roster of M.P.'s who openly declared themselves to be against artificial fluoridation of water supplies. One such M.P. was Mr. Russell Fairgrieve, Conservative member for Aberdeenshire West. As far back as November of 1974 Mr. Fairgrieve had stated his position, which was affirmed in May of 1977, when he again agreed to go on the list of House of Commons members opposed to fluoridation. In June of 1978 he refrained from putting his name on a petition, but wrote to Mr. Blount, "As I have said on many occasions, I would vote against fluoridation if the matter comes up here in parliament ... "

Armed with these assurances, the leader of the Anti-Fluoridation Campaign felt free to inform his members, particularly those resident in the constituency of Aberdeenshire West, that Mr. Russell Fairgrieve was a man who could be trusted to respect their freedom of choice. So following the General Election of May, 1979 Mr. Fairgrieve went back to Westminster with the good wishes of all those who approved his stand on compulsory medication.

In August of 1979, subsequent to his taking up a ministerial post in the new Conservative Government, the M.P. for West Aberdeen was again in correspondence with Clavell Blount, and this time he said, "I have read with great interest the arguments of the pro-fluoride lobby, and more and more I have been convinced of the merits of their case. As you know, I have now been appointed Minister for Health and Social Work at the Scottish Office, and from the evidence I have seen since taking up office, the case for fluoridation would seem to be very strong . . . "

¶131.   A COLLECTIVIST PLOY

Well what about that? The man had changed his standpoint entirely, – and all concurrent with his being given a job in the Home and Health Department. There was no new "evidence" of course, – none that would not have been completely available to Mr. Fairgrieve whether in or out of office. The Department of Health had not been busily researching and evaluating down through the years, so that a new incumbent, with access to its files, might undergo a blinding conversion, as did Paul en route to Damascus. Its views on fluoride, – with all the attendant health risks, – had been fossilised round about 1962, and all Mr. Fairgrieve had done was to bury his own principles in order to establish some kind of rapport with his permanent civil servants.

Coincidentally he had shown that lemming-like characteristic of falling for the wiles of the ideological enemy. For fluoridation just has to be a collectivist ploy, fostered and financed by vested commercial interests on the one hand, and by Fabianised bureaucratic control mania on the other, – in which collusive accord our more perceptive readers will detect the main branches of that complex supra-national conspiracy which for convenience sake has been identified in this volume as THE COMPANY.

¶132.   THE ARROGANCE OF THE
                        MEDICAL ESTABLISHMENT

The fact that so many doctors and dentists are totally convinced of the safety and efficacy of fluoridated water does not in any way detract from the forcible conclusions that have been drawn above. Unless they happen to be specialists in this particular field, they are forced to rely uncritically upon the verdicts and the decisions passed down to them from their professional associations. So why don't the rest of us do likewise, especially mere laymen who can scarcely tell the difference between a steroid and a stethoscope? Why don't we?

Just because it stinks, — stinks of collusion and bureaucratic manipulation, and endorsements of endorsements, and cover-ups, and frantic face-saving exercises by professional bodies and public officials; because the long-standing policy of our health boards, and our dental and medical establishments, — and the conclusions upon which they have based that policy, — are totally at variance with those of their counterparts in France, Germany, Holland, Sweden, Quebec, — sophisticated societies with highly developed public health services, — who have banned fluoride after studying the substantial accumulation of research data concerning its effects upon the human body; because it seems odd that the evidence which appeared convincing to the French, Dutch and Germans should be totally ignored by our Health Ministry and our Royal College of Physicians as they go on insisting that no cases of fluoride poisoning have ever been substantiated; and because with monumental arrogance, and contempt for the ordinary citizen's judgment and perception, they have promoted fluoridation for the masses as an absolute panacea, to the virtual exclusion of instruction and advice upon diet and dental hygiene, which were historically regarded as the only sound basis for healthy teeth. Nary a word nowadays from official sources about sugared fizzy drinks or too

186

many sticky sweeties! Could it be that the confectioners and
the soft drink manufacturers have the ear of the fluoridationist
lobby?

¶133.
FINALLY A MATTER OF ETHICS

All right! by venturing into the fluoridation controversy at
all, one is conscious of having stepped on to a minefield. So
much highly technical medical data! so many statistics which
are subject to widely differing interpretations! But there is one
aspect upon which no true conservative can afford to compromise or equivocate. That is the principle of freedom of choice,
upon which a trusting nation elevated Margaret Thatcher to a
position of supreme political power.

And it is on this aspect that Mr. Russell Fairgrieve, the new
man at the Scottish Home and Health Department, failed himself, his party and his constituents. He could sincerely have
changed his mind upon the merits and de-merits of the assorted
medical data, but not upon that essential sense of moral values
which distinguishes the principled man from the pragmatist, the
ammoral opportunist and the Fabianised manipulator for whom
the end always justifies the means. Deliberately putting a
chemical into the water supply, – for other reasons than to
make it safe and drinkable, – is compulsory medication, and
when the would-be fluoridators claim otherwise, they verbally
tie themselves up in knots. (A comical example of this is repro-
duced on the next page, where a lady member of Mr. Fairgrieve's
staff at the Home and Health Department is endeavouring to
convince a correspondent from the Pure Water Association that
fluoridation cannot be condemned as enforced medication
because fluoride "is not a medicine but a naturally occurring
substance", which "may be added to water to correct a deficiency"; also because fluoridated water would not *only* be used
for "medical purposes", – it would be available for other industrial and domestic purposes, such perhaps as cooling compres-
sors and washing cars.)

Well! well! only an etymological Houdini could help the

187

mf

Scottish Home and Health Department
St Andrew's House Edinburgh EH1 3DE

Telephone 031-556 8501 ext

Mr A G Frame
58 East Main Street
Darvel
Ayrshire

Your reference

Our reference
NJF/7/2/4
Date
11 October 1979

Dear Mr Frame

I refer to your letter of 31 August to
Mr Russell Fairgrieve, to which I have been asked to
reply.

It is not accepted that fluoridation of public water
supplies is medication, enforced or otherwise. Fluoride
is not a medicine but a naturally occurring substance.
It may be added to water to correct a deficiency in the
same way as are many other substances. Fluoridated water
is certainly not wholly or mainly provided for medicinal
purposes. It is supplied for drinking, cleansing or
other domestic and industrial purposes and only incidentally
for the prevention of tooth decay, and the question of
compulsory medication therefore does not arise.

Yours sincerely

SRobertson

MISS S ROBERTSON

lady official escape from the implications of that little lot. But *we* need not be so merciful. We are confronted by evil trends in our society, and the attempt to dispose of a noxious industrial waste into our water supply is only one of them.

So at this moment of time, the henchmen of Mrs. Thatcher were not all doing their bit to combat and ultimately eradicate *the new morality*. In fact, when the enemy came knocking at the gates, one of them, Mr. Russell Fairgrieve, lowered the drawbridge and let them in. What a poor example to the lemming folk, who were badly enough confused beforehand!

THE ORDINARY HONEY BEE, —

in its cross-pollination of fruit and plant life, a humble but indispensable part of man's environment.

In 1979 a Scottish beekeeper opened a new chapter in the fluoride syndrome when he demonstrated that in colder climates honey bees get their winter feeding from a glucose mixture dissolved in water which is usually taken from the domestic supply. The insects are sensitive to even minute quantities of fluoride, and disturbance to their enzyme systems could upset the ecological cycle.

Significantly a Canadian newspaper reported in June of 1979, that in an island on the St. Lawrence River which had been heavily polluted by fluoride emissions from a smelter plant, the bees had disappeared entirely.

CHAPTER SIXTEEN

¶134. Rhodesia — Thatcher Hesitates

One of Mrs. Thatcher's promises whilst in opposition was that she would end the international ostracism of Rhodesia as soon as she was given power to do so. That long-sought opportunity was delayed, — first of all by the personal ambitions of Liberal leader David Steel with his Lib-Lab pact of 1977, — and latterly by Mr. James Callaghan's instincts for clinging to office until the last possible moment. But for these two closely related contingencies, the Thatcher treatment might have been administered some two years earlier, — at a time when it was confidently expected, and in circumstances which were more favourable than those obtaining when she finally reached Downing Street in May of 1979.

As it was, the policies and the tactics which she and her Foreign Secretary were obliged to follow after assuming the responsibilities of government, did not meet with general approval. Many long-time supporters of Rhodesia had hoped that she would see her way to recognise the new Zimbabwe-Rhodesian prime minister Bishop Muzorewa, elected under conditions of universal suffrage during the previous month of April. Rumour has it that she was instinctively inclined to do so, — in which case she would have justified the faith reposed in her by a hard-pressed Salisbury administration, as well as by many thousands of British electors who yearned to see the friendly people of Rhodesia brought back into the family of nations. Had she done so, she might have driven into the open those hidden forces at whose malign presence we have hinted in this volume, — and which were in any case finding it more difficult to maintain their unanimity after the emotive issue of white minority rule had been eliminated. It is also arguable that by showing such strength and resolution she would have demolished much of the potential opposition on the ground, — since strength is still nine-tenths of the argument in the former dark continent of Africa.

¶135.　　　　THE OVERTURNING OF THE
INTERNAL SETTLEMENT

Why did the lady not follow her natural instincts? Who or what persuaded her otherwise? Well, as we shall see later, there could conceivably have been some terrifying pressures. But it was said that she was originally induced to wait until after the Lusaka Conference in July 1979, and that the almost unanimous rejection there of the Rhodesian internal settlement by the assembled delegates from all the Commonwealth countries made her realise the intensity of "world opinion".

At this stage it is necessary to stand back and view that situation with some detachment. Where else in the history of the world had some fifty separate nation states sat down in solemn conclave to discuss the internal affairs of another, — one which had never endeavoured to interfere with the constitutions or lifestyles of its neighbours, and which from a strictly impartial viewpoint was more sinned against than sinning? Even that meddlesome body the U.N. General Assembly was forbidden by charter to discuss other people's internal affairs, and away back in 1966, in the backlash of the U.D.I., was only able to get a debate on Rhodesia at all by having it declared "a threat to peace", — this at a time when the Land of the Flame Lily was the most placid spot in all Southern Africa.

So Margaret Thatcher must have felt she had become part of an Alice in Wonderland scenario when she entered that conference chamber in Lusaka, — though there was nothing fanciful or pantomimish about the work schedule to which she had committed herself and some of her senior colleagues after the tub-thumping and rhetoric was over. The convening in London of a new session of constitutional talks, to which would be invited representatives of all the Zimababwe-Rhodesian factions including the Salisbury administration, the internal political parties and the guerrillas operating in the bush! In due course, pressure upon Bishop Muzorewa to renounce his premiership, and the Salisbury Parliament to vote for its own dissolution, so that the country could have the temporary status of a Crown Colony under a British governor! Reduction of the European seats in the proposed new parliament from twenty-eight to twenty, so that the whites would no longer be able to block any discriminatory legislation aimed at diminishing or abolishing their special status! Hopefully the negotiation of a cease-fire in the bush war, with the stand-down of the Rhodesian security forces, and confinement in hastily improvised assembly camps for the guerrillas! Finally, a re-run of the elections of April 1979, only this time with the guerrilla chiefs of the oddly assorted Patriotic Alliance taking a major part! The fate of a nation placed once again in the hands of an unsophisticated black electorate, which would be subject to terror, intimidation and mass emotionalism at being involved in a process which had not caught on anywhere else in emergent Africa, — the very situation which Ian Smith had warned against, and had given fourteen years of his life to try and avoid!

A COUNTRY THROWN BACK INTO TURMOIL

¶136.

Six months after Lusaka, it was all happening. Lord Soames installed as Queen's representative and Governor at Salisbury's Marimba House! The Union Jack flying on flagstaffs whence it had been pulled down in anger and disappointment some ten years previously! British Tommies, recently dropped on the tarmac at Salisbury Airport, cautiously filtering out into the bush, along dirt roads that had hopefully been swept clear of mines! A gradual liaison building up with the battle-hardened Rhodesian security forces, who knew the terrain and the terrorists' tricks! Guerrillas moving tentatively into the ceasefire reception camps, the trickle swelling into a flood, *mugibva* informers joining in from the kraals, and hoping to be mistaken for fighting men as detachments of the ZANLA faction stayed outside the supervisory cordon for future Africa-style electioneering activities! Nation and administrators alike facing a situation that had no known precedents, as hastily organised political parties embarked upon weeks of noisy and sometimes violent campaigning, whilst commercial and industrial decisions stood suspended upon a ballot-box verdict that could easily portend anarchy and civil war! An influx of Liberal internationalist pressmen, — many of them on COMPANY expense accounts, — enjoying the uncertainty and confusion, wishing aloud for a Marxist victory, and losing no opportunity to celebrate the end of U.D.I.! T.V. reporters shoving microphones under the noses of passers-by in Jameson Avenue, and asking them if the fourteen years of sanctions, world-wide ostracism and guerrilla war had all been worthwhile!

REMINISCENCES OF THE ECONOMIC AND PSYCHOLOGICAL WAR

¶137.

Well, had it been worthwhile? And who was most qualified to provide the answer? Some of those newsmen and broadcasters seemed scarcely old enough to know how it all started. The break up of the Federation! The promises made to successive Rhodesian governments by a Fabian-orientated Whitehall which always saw the goal of independence as being somewhere round the corner! The vacillations! The changing attitudes! The to-ing and fro-ing! The advance and retreat psychosis, as each concession on the part of the Rhodesians was used as a handhold to urge them one step further on! The perfidy of solemn agreements thwarted by subtle re-phrasing or the insertion of the small print! In the Britain of the nineteen-sixties not one person in ten thousand would understand how a perverted Fabian bureaucracy went about the attainment of its devious ends. How many therefore were able to appreciate the feeling of mistrust and exasperation which had finally prompted the U.D.I.?

And after the U.D.I.? Britain's prime minister Harold Wilson, breathing sound and fury, promising that Ian Smith's rebel government would be brought down in weeks rather than months! Whitehall's spiteful mandarins eagerly preparing for the most thoroughly reprehensible campaign that had ever been waged against our own bloodstock since the war with the American colonies in 1776! The beginning of that era of petty vindictiveness during which loyal servants of the Crown, men who had served their Sovereign with distinction in two world wars, were banned from our shores, whilst our international airports continued to admit the scum of the earth, from revolutionary terrorists to I.R.A. bombers! The Royal Navy (shame on its honoured traditions) pressed into service for a blockade upon the Mozambique seaport of Beira, hopefully that the Rhodesian economy might be immobilised through lack of oil! Trade sanctions against the supply of Rhodesian tobacco and various strategic materials, including a superior quality of chrome, for which the only alternative source was Soviet Russia! To venture further into this realm of sanctions and boycotts is to go with Alice through the Looking Glass into that topsy-turvy world which even a succinct and perspicacious Lewis Carroll did not expect to encounter other than in pantomime'

¶138. HOW THE U.N. DENIED RHODESIA A HEARING

But was this campaign of spite and vindictiveness the work of Britain's Fabianised civil servants alone? Was it an end-product of incredible ignorance by Harold Wilson, his Socialist ministers and his misfit of a Colonial Secretary about the realities of Africa? A purely domestic quarrel as between a parent nation and a rebellious offspring to which it had been attempting to apply a measure of restraint and discipline? Not so! Wilson would get the blame of having "internationalised" the Rhodesian imbroglio, but the fact of the matter was that it had been made a global issue with or without his compliance. All through 1966 and 1967 the United Nations General Assembly was very much preoccupied with debates and resolutions upon the continuing resistance of Rhodesia to trade

195

sanctions and all the other associated pressures, and a feature of the proceedings was the repetitive demand that the "insurrection" should be put down by the use of force.

Here again we find ourselves in that topsy-turvy land beyond the Looking Glass. For where else in recent history had the world body felt itself empowered to advise and criticise a member state for its handling of an alleged insurgency within its territories? Had it happened when Pandit Nehru set out to subdue the Naga hill tribes? or when the northern Arabs committed genocide against the negroes of the Southern Sudan? or when Julius Nyerere started liquidating the "dissident" elements on the offshore island of Zanzibar? or indeed in any one of a dozen satanic principalities where despotic savagery was exacting a dreadful toll in human misery? So why, why, why in Rhodesia, where a tolerant white race, caught in the backlash of the "wind of change", provided peace and security for an assortment of tribal peoples in a spirit of old-fashioned paternalism? Why also, when on the 11th October 1967, the President of the International Council for Rhodesia had petitioned to the Fourth Committee of the U.N. General Assembly for the Rhodesian case to be presented before them, had the committee rejected his request by sixty-six votes to one? The world body, the future parliament of mankind, denying the accused party even the courtesy of a hearing! An international court, sitting in arbitration upon the fate of an entire population, — and regulating its business on the well-established principles of kangaroo justice, — that the judgment should be made before the trial, and the execution, for preference, before the judgment!

DOUGLAS REED AND THE
¶139. MASTER PLAN FOR SOUTHERN AFRICA

Why Rhodesia? Douglas Reed, the political satirist who had striven so hard to warn us against the rise of Hitlerism in the 1930's, and who had been equally prescient about the Soviet menace that would follow, pointed the way to some of the answers when he wrote "The Battle for Rhodesia" in 1966. Having enjoyed in his earlier years the Cassandra-like distinction

196

of alerting his contemporaries to "little countries, far away", which would subsequently become the turning-point for world events, Reed now showed that in the 1966 context that "little country" was post-U.D.I. Rhodesia, and his exposure of a Grand Design or Master Plan for the internationalisation of the entire sub-continent of Southern Africa caught the attention of men of vision all over the Western Hemisphere, men who could lift their eyes from the bustle and trivialities of everyday, and look occasionally to the hills.

What they saw there was not entirely to their liking. The gist of Reed's message was that once again the civilised world was drifting into something corrupt and potentially very unpleasant, that the surreptitious pressures that were then threatening to crush Rhodesian independence could be menacing the American Middle West or the European heartland a decade or two further on, — that what happened in Salisbury's Milton Buildings, or in her tobacco and metal markets, or on her vital trade routes down to the Indian Ocean, — or to the morale, the will power and the general wellbeing of all her assorted races, — was important to the denizen of Whitehall or Washington, Wisconsin or Worcestershire, Wigan or Wilmington or Winnipeg; that they could not escape it, no matter how far away they might be.

¶140. IAN SMITH UPSETS THE TIME-TABLE

Thus the battle for Rhodesia was slipping into its proper perspective. Those who have stayed the course all the way in this study of the lemming folk will have become wise and philosophical on such matters, — will therefore find no difficulty in appreciating that what Ian Douglas Smith and his cabinet colleagues had done away back there in 1965 was to upset an important COMPANY timetable. They had stood foursquare in the path of "progress" and "liberalisation", and the future development of the New World Order, and as such they became targets of abuse and vilification from the four corners of the globe.

Perhaps at the time few of them realised the enormity of what they had done. Lord Graham, the former Duke of Montrose, Minister of Defence in Smith's first Rhodesian Front government, and one of the senior signatories to the Independence Declaration, told the author in 1972 that he himself had expected the whole affair to blow over in a few years at most. We know now, of course, that could never be allowed to happen. THE COMPANY and its agents were appalled at the prospect of a conservative white race sitting indefinitely astride both the mineral wealth and the infiltration routes for social and political subversion, — and having limitless funds at their disposal, *were always able to recruit parties and factions who would thwart any kind of political settlement with the existing power structure in Salisbury.*

¶141.

A FINANCIAL FALLACY EXPOSED

Ostensibly the campaign of mandatory sanctions was being waged against a perpetuation of white minority rule. But judging by their performance elsewhere, those international power brokers who financed it were not all that much concerned about racial dignity or increasing the sum of human happiness. For them there just *had* to be something else.

And indeed there *was* a subtle aspect of the Rhodesian situation which would never hit the headlines, no matter how many thousands of words were spoken or written about it. The fact was that after full financial and economic sanctions had been brought into effect, including expulsion from the Sterling Area and a freezing of loans and credit facilities throughout the world banking community, — after Rhodesia had become a non-country whose passports, currency and diplomacy were not recognised anywhere except in neighbouring South Africa, — the financiers had a problem. The measures which they had enacted were confidently calculated to bring the defiant Ian Smith to his knees. When they failed to do so, when on the contrary the Rhodesian economy started to flourish and expand under sanctions, there was all the dismay and consternation of the angler who sees his prize fish getting away. Worse! there was also a looming danger that other bigger fish might slip the hook and enjoy the taste of freedom.

Nations are controlled these days, not necessarily by force of arms, but by a stranglehold upon their sources of credit. The postwar era of de-colonisation saw many small and relatively impoverished states achieving political independence, bestowed upon them with varying degrees of grace and enthusiasm by their former imperial masters. As was earlier suggested in "The Mind Benders", that sort of independence is seldom any threat to the financial power structure, since it is usually accompanied by massive development loans which have to be serviced and monitored, often with the attachment of strings which keep the embryo state securely anchored within the orbit. Few of the new nations which clamoured to join the U.N. in the post-colonial period have ever been completely out of hock since they paid the bill for their independence celebrations.

¶142.   SCOTLAND AND SOCIAL CREDIT

The argument of that deep-sighted Scots engineer C.H. Douglas was that any state which could be seen to flourish outwith the rules and restrictions of the existing money system would automatically expose that system's fallacies and iniquities, and bring about a revolution in conventional financial thinking. It is not generally known that within the ranks of the Scottish independence movement there are a number of Douglas's disciples who, when they saw the prospect of national autonomy, began to visualise a significant role for their own small country. To them Scotland seemed just big enough and sufficiently well endowed to do it, — to break the stranglehold of collectivist philosophy and centralised bureaucracy, and within her own borders provide a forum for those unorthodox monetary ideas which were being stifled in the wider world outside. The nation which had produced Thomas Robertson and C.H. Douglas was not lacking in the wit and expertise with which to order its financial affairs in pointed exclusion of the World Bank and International Monetary Fund, — a development which might have seen its sponsors cast in the same heretical mould as the Rhodesians, when they incurred the wrath of a manipulated world opinion. (It was to provide an informed background for this hypothetical situation that "The Mind Benders" addressed itself to the prospects and problems of Scottish independence in a western world increasingly threatened by Marxist-collectivist takeover.)

¶143. THE REAL CAUSE OF THE AMERICAN WARS OF INDEPENDENCE?

Historical writers who *refuse* to ignore the influence that monetary policies have played in our troubled past are now tending more and more to put a new interpretation upon some of the most dramatic and well-known episodes of ancient and modern history. For instance, in "The Babylonian Woe", David Astle, British patriot and wartime naval officer, points out that the phenomenal prosperity enjoyed by the American colonies up to the mid-seventeen-sixties was due to the fact that they were in entire control of their own currency, which they called Colonial Scrip, and which was issued according to the demands of their own trade and industry. Astle quotes United States Senator Robert L. Owen as testifying that this idyllic state of affairs ended when the British Parliament passed legislation which prohibited any colony from creating its own credit. As a result the colonists had to go to the Bank of England, where their home-based scrip issues were withdrawn and replaced with English money provided on the orthodox system of debit-financing, — but at such a poor rate of exchange that within one year of the monetary realignment, unemployment and misery were rife on the New England seaboard. This, according to Owen, was the real cause of the American revolution and the independence wars that followed, — the more publicised issues, such as the Boston tea party, being for the delight and distraction of the multitude.

Where else in our modern history were there examples of states or societies which had flourished in defiance of the accepted financial conventions? What about Nazi Germany in the nineteen-thirties, before the irrevocable commitment to another world war? It was said then that Hitler could not possibly survive since he had incurred the hostility of the international financial community, and had thereby forfeited the privilege of raising external credits. His much vaunted rearmament plans were hailed with derision in London and New York. His tanks were armoured with *papier-mâché*, and the children of the Third Reich were growing up deformed and stunted because their totalitarian government had opted for guns before butter. Such was the aura of indispensability with which the orthodox financial mechanisms had invested themselves that these stories and arguments were given undue credence at the time. People had been conditioned to accept that no sophisticated society or enterprise could possibly survive or develop outwith the constraints of conventional monetary rectitude.

Subsequent events were to prove all this fallacious nonsense. Despite being isolated by the international financial community, Germany not only built up the world's most formidable fighting machine, she also manned it with tough young Aryan fanatics who had thrived so well on austerity that in twelve months of impressive conquest their shiny jackboot heels were arrogantly planted upon a prostrate continent of Europe. All right! it was all based upon a bent and destructive philosophy. But did Hitler have to invade Poland in the autumn of 1939? And what prompted him to massacre the little defenceless people of European Jewry?

·The author has neither space nor competence with which to dwell upon these questions. But judging by our experience in other matters, it may be that the true answers are not what we have traditionally accepted.

SPARKING OFF A
¶144.   CONSERVATIVE REVIVAL

Back now to a Rhodesia which had been smitten with the full weight of mandatory U.N. sanctions, which had been thrown out of the Sterling Area, and whose bank loans and credit facilities had been frozen in all the money markets of the sophisticated industrial and commercial world! This was the stage at which, under the conventional rules, her economy should have started to wilt and wither, and her erstwhile proud and defiant rulers to crawl on their bended knees as suppliants before a modestly triumphant financial establishment.

The problem was that things did not seem to be tending in that direction at all. With a self-sufficiency in food, vast reserves of strategic minerals, a conservative policy of extraction and exploitation, and a vigorous free enterprise economy, the Rhodesians were not only surviving sanctions, — they gave clear indication that if ever the external pressures were removed, their country's stability and prosperity would make it the hub of trade and investment for all Central Africa.

Meanwhile the spirited resistance of one little country to what many perceptive souls had recognised as unjust and sinister international pressures, kindled imaginations far and wide, and sparked off a conservative revival in corners where its few remaining embers had all but been extinguished by the prevailing flood of liberalism. Salisbury became the Mecca of mainly Rightist thinkers who had watched their own countries brought low by successive doses of collectivism and internationalism, and who thought they saw in the indomitable figure of Ian Smith a symbol of that Anglo-Saxon courage and resolution which had been only too common before the Western World started to lose its soul. Friends of Rhodesia associations sprang up in South Africa, America, Australia, New Zealand, Canada, Scotland, France, West Germany, Portugal and even such outlandish spots as Taiwan and South Korea, — everywhere one found people who had become depressed and disorientated by prevailing social and political trends, and who needed a focal point for their resistance. Douglas Reed's warning was being heeded, — if not by the mass of humanity, at least by that intellectual band who would set a new pattern for the future. It was being realised that men of conscience and foresight could simply not afford to ignore evil and corruption and double-dealing just because it was not happening on their own doorsteps. There was a great meeting of minds and a coming-together of ideas during those years, and it was all happening because in November of 1965 one man had had the courage to stand up and say, "So far and no further."

Many of those minds were clever and well-trained, accustomed to evaluating effects and causes. Many also had brought with them more than a passing knowledge of international intrigue and subversion, — and the contrast of life in Rhodesia as they observed it, with the caricatures which were nightly portrayed on the Western World's T.V. screens, told them all too clearly that they had stumbled upon another COMPANY ploy. For them the little country between the Zambezi and the Limpopo had become the frontier of civilisation as they knew it, — the embattled outpost where a resolute few would buy time whilst the rest of their kind were awakening from a hypnotic slumber.

"MAINLY A QUESTION OF REFUGEES"

¶ 145.

THE COMPANY was having its methods and some of its agents exposed in this unexpectedly difficult affair in Central Africa, but there was absolutely no prospect of it ever going away and forgetting about the whole business. Pressures on the Smith Government vastly increased after the revolution in Portugal, which resulted in Communist regimes for both Angola and Mozambique, and the addition of hundreds of miles of potentially hostile frontier. Dr. Kissinger, who did a brief spell of shuttle diplomacy in 1974, got the stubborn Rhodesian premier to agree to the inevitability of majority African rule, and though it was several troubled and war-scarred years later that he made his compact with the internal nationalist leaders, they had been years of unrelenting international pressure, with no apparent end in sight. Even the election of Bishop Muzorewa by popular vote in April of 1979 had done nothing to allay the bitterness and mistrust at the U.N., where the Security Council unanimously declared the Rhodesian poll null and void, and called upon all member nations to continue the policy of sanctions. Why?

It was just that some conditions had not been satisfied. The guerrilla leaders N'Komo and Mugabe, though offered immunity and a safe conduct, had chosen not to contest the 1979 election, since they had no desire to fight a political campaign in which they did not control the levers of administrative power. Also, some of Rhodesia's most virulent critics felt that the original architects of U.D.I. were getting off too lightly. They felt cheated without the show trials and summary executions which were the stuff and substance of revolution elsewhere in Africa, — and it was in fact revolution that they had always wanted.

The One World Monopolists who directed the affairs of THE COMPANY had also set their hearts upon a revolution. They had given their backing to the Anglo-American initiative of September 1977, a principal clause of which was that the Rhodesian security forces would be disbanded, and their responsibilities handed over to the guerrillas who had been perpetrating the atrocities in the bush. It was a sure recipe for civil war, since the two rival factions of the ill-assorted Patriotic Front Alliance were rent by tribal differences that could easily develop into a fight. So if the much heralded plan cobbled together by the British Fabian David Owen and the American Marxist Andrew Young had ever been put into operation, there would eventually have been little left but the pieces.

This sort of end-play had a particular appeal for THE COMPANY, since it meant that they would get rid of Rhodesia's whites. Dr. Kissinger had first brought this aspect of Establishment thinking to the forefront when he declared that in the ultimate the Rhodesian problem was "mainly a question of refugees". Approximately a year later John Davies, then Conservative Shadow Foreign Secretary, returned from a visit to Salisbury obsessed with the need to requisition a fleet of airliners that would uplift a possible 180,000 people, — so he also had caught on to the theme about the refugees. Young and Owen between them, if they had got away with their Anglo-American plan, would certainly have fixed it for him though whether the whites fled in Davis's chartered airliners or chose to be slaughtered where they stood, it would have made little difference to the two conspiratorial scarecrows, so long as they were got out of the way. For it seemed that *until* they were got out of the way, there were some deep-laid schemes which could not be brought to fruition.

WHAT CHANCE A MULTI-RACIAL DEMOCRACY?

¶146.

So the question which arises at this stage is to what extent the Carrington-Thatcher last ditch settlement will have thwarted THE COMPANY's master plan for Southern Africa. Will the whites feel encouraged to go on living and working in the land which their ancestors developed out of the African bush, — or will they drift gradually away to be replaced by ex-patriates whose interest in the country might be limited to what they could extract from it during the terms of their contracts?

The author is simply not willing to be dragged into futile conjecture. Neither has he much heart for dwelling upon the ramifications of one-skull one-vote African politics. It may be that the mutual respect and tolerance, the happy spirit of co-operation, the sense of human dignity and sympathetic understanding which developed between Rhodesians of all races during the years of sanctions and ostracism, will somehow survive the baleful influence of the international meddlers and go on to build that multiracial democracy which thus far has only existed in the realms of Whitehall Fabiana.

Who knows? If it works now, as it has never worked anywhere else in Africa, even the cynics amongst us will be truly thankful. Whatever else it may have done, the Lancaster House agreement has apparently put an end to an increasingly bloody and protracted guerrilla war, and those who saw the ravages of that war at first hand had no right to expect that Rhodesians, both black and white, should go on bleeding and suffering indefinitely whilst the outside world looked on with callous indifference and a frightening degree of ignorance about the momentous issues that were involved.

¶147.   THE ADVOCATES OF FEDERATION

From about 1970 onwards, there were in white Rhodesian politics an increasing number of uncompromising activists who saw, in Ian Smith's efforts to reach an internationally acceptable settlement, a gradualist surrender to the very forces which U.D.I. had been intended to contain. These people, most of whom were, or had been, stalwarts in the ruling Rhodesian Front Party, tended to take the view that their country was much safer in isolation than it could ever be in dubious negotiations with the madding world outside. They found a reporter and a spokesman in Wilfred Brooks, the articulate editor of *Rhodesian Property & Finance*, who became more and more critical of the Prime Minister and his policies with every month that passed, till he was ultimately depicting the legendary Smithy as a sort of Fifth Columnist for the Internationalist Brigade who were always waiting in the wings.

The insistent message spelled out by this stoical and determined pressure group was that from her entrenched position, with the trust and cooperation of the hereditary chiefs and no great clamour for precipitate change from the mass of the indigenous population, Rhodesia could only be defeated by Rhodesians themselves. Feelers towards a "settlement", trimming of principles, infringements of selectivity and the breakdown of what were regarded as essential white standards, were all condemned as weaknesses which would inevitably be used to force more and more concessions. The group's own long-term solution was a form of separate development such as was already being implemented in South Africa. They saw for each racial entity the prospect of "government by its own kind", and for the country at large a federation loosely held together by a central administration in Salisbury. After the failure of the Pearce Commission in 1972, the federal option was being actively canvassed and investigated from within the Prime Minister's own office, and in an atmosphere where such experiments could have been tried and tested away from the inhibiting influence of an orchestrated world opinion, it is just possible that a Federated States of Rhodesia would have come into being.

But in the prevailing circumstances it was never a practical proposition. The survival game for the ruling caucus of the Rhodesian Front was now to watch that nothing was said or done that would prejudice the prospects of a settlement. People had become conditioned to the belief that whilst Smithy kept the promise of that eventual "settlement" dangling in front of the international community, the external enemy would stay his hand, and the skies would not be allowed to fall. And since Smithy was the man in the hot seat, few were willing to risk supplanting him with an untried newcomer. His personal power increased with every passing year, till Ivor Richards was prompted to boast that he was strong enough to push through any agreement on black majority rule in the face of any political opposition.

And what of his accusers, those who claimed that he and his administration were fighting a no-win war against the terrorists, and that it was his constant backtracking in search of a settlement which was paralysing the decision-making sectors of the economy and stepping up the emigration losses? Wilfred Brooks and his business journal were financially ruined in June of 1977 when judgment was given against them for a personal libel on the Prime Minister with respect to the Sithole kidnapping incident. Many of the others, including one or two of the original signatories to the U.D.I. of 1965, departed the country within the following eighteen months when it was obvious that black majority rule would not be delayed much longer. Their names, and the parts they played, may soon be lost to history, but they are mentioned here as stubborn opponents of "the wind of change" who understood perhaps better than the bulk of their countrymen the international forces with which they were contending, and who yet were willing to go to the brink of disaster and beyond, before they would compromise their beliefs or their principles.

All right! so the entire population was not comprised of battle-hardened iconoclasts who had learned the implications of

207

the Master Plan, and were bitter against it happening in Rhodesia. There were also hundreds of thousands of ordinary folk who had had enough of fighting and terror and international ostracism, and when there finally arrived in Britain a government which offered to lend a helping hand, – instead of the diatribes in Marxist-Fabianism which they had been used to hearing from the previous lot, – they pulled down their defences, both physical and psychological, and let the newcomers in.

COMPANY PREFERENCES FOR REVOLUTION

It subsequently emerged of course that they could still get Marxist-Fabianism, for their electoral fate had been put in the care of honest chaps from Billericay and Bermondsey who were adept at controlling the polling for the local city council, but had had no previous experience of *mugibvas*, and how they could be used in outlying kraals and tribal districts to get a one hundred per cent turn out in favour of the new-style witch doctors who practised socialist revolution.

Strange how those sophisticated Western societies and their worldly wise politicians, who had exposed the deficiencies and the ineptitudes of socialism in their own countries, were still not unwilling to have its brutal repressive code of unenlightened authoritarianism thrust upon the poor half-educated masses of emergent Africa, – like the lord and lady of the manor sorting out their old discarded clothes, and handing them down to be worn and gawked upon by the simple peasants in the village!

Those who may still respond with avid cynicism to our illustrative concept of THE COMPANY as a conspiratorial organisation which operates on both sides of the political spectrum, should ponder why, in the changing conditions of Southern Africa, it is invariably the extremist solution which is canvassed, encouraged, financed and promoted in all the organs and outlets of a manipulated world opinion. Marxist regimes were promptly recognised and supported in Mozambique and Angola, to the exclusion and effacement of a long-headed democratically-orientated character like Dr. Savimbi. In South-West Africa the settlement proposals have been interminably bedevilled by United Nations predilections and shameless bias in favour of a revolutionary terrorist called Sam Nujoma, and at à sensitive period in 1978 the eighty-six non-aligned Third World countries decided to help things along by admitting his SWAPO guerrilla organisation to full membership of their movement. Likewise with Rhodesia the men with the guns and the inflammatory rhetoric were always more likely to get a sympathetic hearing from the U.N. and the world's press than those who preached moderation and non-violence. Surely it points to the assumption that only through revolution, through a complete breakdown and subversion of the existing societies, can THE COMPANY and its hidden persuaders gain their devious ends.

So even under a settlement master-minded by the British aristocrat Lord Carrington, and vetted and supervised by the staunchly conservative Margaret Thatcher, what does this mean for Rhodesia?

¶149.　　　　ORIGINS OF ZIMBABWE

It means first of all that the new independent state will not be known as Rhodesia at all, — that the name of Cecil Rhodes is scheduled to be erased from the map of Africa. Thenceforth the land will be known as Zimbabwe, in recognition of a romantic old pile of ruins situated about ten miles south of Fort Victoria, and much debated and investigated by archaeologists since its discovery by elephant hunters in the latter half of the nineteenth century. Here we have to note how a cruel deception has been practised upon the early nationalists who aspired to create a black nation out of the various tribal peoples settled on the plains between the Zambezi and the Limpopo. For their Fabian mentors had encouraged them to believe that the various *zimbabwes* or *houses of stone* whose impressive ruins could still be detected in isolated corners of Rhodesia were vestiges of an ancient Bantu culture and civilisation reaching back to the early centuries of the Christian era.

It was a classic example of Fabian guff and inverted

The Acropolis at Great Zimbabwe,
with Lake Kyle in the distance.

thinking, where the facts are tailored to suit the hypothesis. It was also an unlikely canard, since the Bantu peoples had never shown any ability or inclination for building in stone during the authenticated eras of their history, — and the construction of the citadel at Great Zimbabwe is a masterpiece of dry stone building which would do honour to the master masons of this or any other generation of craftsmen. As such, it had initially been quite properly identified as the product of a European or Near Eastern culture, with a slant in favour of the Arab races who traded in and out of Sofala and Mogadishu in pre-mediaeval times, and who had presumably gone prospecting up the Sabi and Lundi Rivers in search of gold.

Robert Gayre, the far-travelled Scottish ethnologist and archaeologist, makes the impressive point that according to carbon isotope half-life datings, the latest constructional work round the walled settlement at Great Zimbabwe took place at or near the end of the fifteenth century. This coincided with the voyages of exploration round the Cape of Good Hope by the adventurous Vasco da Gama, and the eventual capture of Sofala by the Portuguese in 1507. Arab goldminers, exploiting their finds in the upper reaches of the Tokwe River, were likely to be instantly affected by the loss of their supply port to the advance detachments of a colonising power. On the other hand a supposed Bantu empire occupying the great central African interior, and based on southern Mashonaland, would be as much impacted by the activities of Portuguese seafarers as were the sparse inhabitants of the Gobi Desert when the first astronauts went to the moon.

It was all so phony, — as phony as the social sciences and Keynesian economics and the Marxist-socialist Nirvana. It had no evidence, either cultural, technical or scientific with which to support it, only the urge to manufacture a myth which would further THE COMPANY's plans in Southern Africa. But after several decades of African schoolchildren on day or weekend outings had hopped and skipped their way round the Zimbabwe Ruins, on the say-so of their suitably indoctrinated schoolmarms that they were looking upon the works of mighty and illustrious ancestors, where was the re-writing of history likely to end? And was it a good omen for the new state to base its name upon a piece of archaeological sophistry?

¶150.   CONSERVATIVES TAKE
                     THE SURRENDER

Thatcher had come and conquered where Wilson, Callaghan and Owen had failed. The sanctions which at times had seemed immovable and insurmountable, had effectively disappeared as a result of a bill hurriedly pushed through the Westminster parliament in December of 1979. Enormous risks would be contemplated as the electoral process, so foreign to tribal Africa, was put into practice in an atmosphere of fear, mistrust, intimidation and ages old superstition. Hopefully the honest chaps from Billericay and Bermondsey would catch on to the terror tactics of Africa-style electioneering, and would strive to eliminate the worst abuses. But it was always a perilous and unpredictable exercise which the country-born Rhodesian, from the depths of his own experience, would fain have avoided at all costs.

In the end he had no choice. Insidious and persistent international pressures, unswervingly supported by the lemming folk of many nations, progressively eroded the proud position which he had rightly enjoyed as a civiliser and an emancipator in a once savage land. Not for the first time in the context of Africa, it had fallen upon a British Conservative government to administer the *coup de grace*. Thatcher and her envoys had been able to get agreement, compliance, — even surrender, — after the Fabians Crosland and Owen had been avoided like the plague. Union Jacks! O.H.M.S.! ER II official cars! A Queen's Governor back at Marimba House! And a T.V. reporter out with a microphone in Jameson Avenue, asking the passers-by whether it had all been worthwhile!

Well! *you* tell him, you who have been through it all, — and have experienced things which can neither be forgiven nor forgotten. It may ultimately be accepted that THE COMPANY has paid dearly for this long delayed victory in Central Africa, that the over-exposure of its agencies and its methods will have created such a feeling of awareness as to make further progress on these lines impossible. And it will all have happened because a tiny segment of the Anglo-Saxon race, mercifully isolated from the Fabian-collectivist disease which had paralysed and inhibited their more numerous kinsfolk in the Northern Hemisphere, had both the vigour and the courage to stand up and be counted at a time when there were so few to answer the call. The battle for Rhodesia was over. Like all battles, it had produced its casualties and its heroes. But no one who had played the smallest part in the events of those fourteen years of U.D.I. would ever have any right to say that it should not have happened. The world was potentially a better place after Rhodesia had fought and lost, than it might have been if she had not fought at all.

¶151.   A RETURN TO ORTHODOX
                        FINANCE

But what's this stuff about fighting and losing? Was this what the Thatcher-Carrington settlement would ultimately be, – defeat and humiliation? If the country somehow survived the shambles and violence of African one-man-one-vote elections, and some sort of stable government emerged, – if the free enterprise system remained essentially intact, and the white population stayed on to operate it with their customary drive and efficiency, – if development money poured in from abroad so that trade and banking flourished, and the white municipalities of Salisbury and Bulawayo became the commercial and communications axis of Central Africa, – if the newly forged links with a Conservative Britain remained strong, and her moderating influence persisted, so that it no longer looked as if Julius Nyerere was ever going to get his socialist dream of a Marxist confederacy poised on the banks of the Limpopo, – if all these prospects came up to their most optimistic expectations, might that not be regarded as something of a victory?

Well, maybe! But remember that THE COMPANY had originally wanted bloody revolution, – and even if Margaret

213

Thatcher had apparently persuaded them to settle for less, it did not mean that they would not try again. They were not likely to forget the economic miracle which the Rhodesians had performed in those years of U.D.I., when despite an international embargo, despite having their credit facilities frozen, despite being thrown out of the Sterling Area and the world's money markets, they had expanded their trade, doubled and varied their food production, and fostered a light engineering and industrial infra-structure that might never have developed under any other circumstances.

This was not all. The Rhodesian dollar, which started life on par with the ten shilling note, — and which Harold Wilson, upon the best of banking advices, had declared to be virtually worthless, — had steadily risen in value during the first seven or eight years of U.D.I., till it peaked at about eighty-two pence in sterling money, an appreciation of approximately sixty-four per cent. So as a consequence of being kicked out of the international financial system, the Rhodesians had not only found the will and the means to expand and diversify their economy, they had also insulated themselves from the worst effects of world inflation.

It was a situation which would not be allowed to endure for long after the settlement. The development money which had been so long denied would now be readily available at rates between twelve and seventeen per cent, and with a new black majority government committed to enlarged spending programmes, there would be little resistance to a resumption of orthodox financial practice. From the viewpoint of THE COMPANY, a dangerous experiment had been terminated. Whoever acceded to power in Salisbury, it was unlikely that they would be either willing or able to issue their own Colonial Scrip.

CHAPTER SEVENTEEN

¶152. The Mechanism of World Turmoil

What is the surest way of maintaining peace in our time? By building up the most sophisticated defences known to modern technology? or by adopting a low and passive posture?

In October of 1979 Mr. Francis Pym, Defence Secretary in the Thatcher Government, was pledging an updating of the Polaris submarine missile force so that it would remain fully effective into the 1990's, — and General Sir Walter Walker, a former commander of NATO, was telling a British Israel Congress that the West would have to re-arm rapidly if it did not wish to find its sources of vital raw materials threatened by the Soviets in the Middle East, South-East Asia and Southern Africa.

Forthright generals like Sir Walter Walker, and *hawkish* politicians like Francis Pym, are deplored by those moderate middle-of-the-road chaps who would never go so far as to say that we should disarm unilaterally, yet who faithfully supported the last Labour Government as it quietly and surreptitiously ran down our defence capability to the stage where, outside of Europe, we could scarcely have mounted a strike against a modern pirates' lair, and even in Europe there were serious logistic worries about how long the wheels would keep turning, how long the guns could keep firing.

So who would we prefer running our defence establishment? Fire eaters like General Walker? or Liberal smoothies

215

who would see that the blunt end was well padded out at the expense of the sharp end? Guns without firing pins, or short on ammunition! Cannons into ploughshares! Commandos into armchair bureaucrats or war office doorkeepers! What a commendable prospect in a world so secure and peaceful that armament was a superfluous charge upon the public purse!

But neither Francis Pym nor Sir Walter Walker believe that we live in such a world, — and it so happens that these men are realists. Yet the sort of high technology re-armament which they advise comes in multi-million pound packages, — and as soon as figures are mentioned, the smoothies start reckoning up the cost in terms of hospital beds and National Health prescriptions. All as if the energy, know-how and technology channelled into one project, would — once discarded — automatically beam on to welfare production of the other.

¶153.   THE HIGH PRICE OF HIGH
                    TREASON

We are not involved in a costly armaments race because of realists like Francis Pym or fire-eaters like General Walker. We are there because Marxist-Fabians in the American Establishment have been transferring high military technology to the Russians for a terrifying period of years, and because our own security and intelligence organisations have been so riddled with the same kind of Marxist-Fabian subversion that the nation's most vital secrets were at risk as soon as they were fed into the system. Yes, the Blunt-MacLean-Burgess and Kim Philby syndrome! How many more MacLeans, Philbys and Burgesses, — and how many of them are still at it? Even under the Thatcher Government is there any sign yet of the patriotic scourge that will be necessary to flush the slimy creatures and their abnormal desires out of our security system, and replace them with men and women of trust? In the broader social sphere, is there indeed any sign of rising revulsion against the Marxist-Liberal complex which allows traitors and treachery to be fostered so tolerantly in our midst?

Armaments race? Who in their right minds ever wanted it

to happen this way? But if we don't restore an effective strike capability, — if we don't recover both the will power and the strength with which to secure our lifelines and our access to strategic materials, all the hospital beds and National Health pills that ever existed won't preserve us from either incineration or a dark age of collectivist tyranny. After all, when the Khmer Rouge took over in Pnom Penh, they *cleared* the hospitals, beds, bed-ridden patients and all, and sent them trundling on a long dusty trek to nowhere. Do we ever want to place our nation and our people in that position, so that by the whim of a new Stalinesque bureaucracy, the same kind of spectacle can be re-enacted in London or Glasgow or Manchester?

¶154.   MONITORING THE OTHER ARM
OF THE NUTCRACKER

But adequate re-armament, a sharpening of our strike weapons, a thickening of our defensive armour, is only one half of our philosophical re-alignment. The other half is to develop a fuller understanding of that financial-capitalist-monopolist-cum-subversive and revolutionary mechanism which for convenience we have called THE COMPANY.

It was necessary to bring all the tricks, contrivances and many-sided manipulations of THE COMPANY into this volume about the lemming folk, because without an appreciation of its vast ramifications one is totally unable to comprehend why the insidious attack upon our democratic freedoms comes from both extremities of the spectrum. Like the two jaws of a nut-cracker, in fact!

Those lonely but dedicated souls who explore the failures and fallacies of our money system keep trying to warn us that it is the international financiers, the credit-debit ledger page manipulators, who in their ceaseless search for more and more absolute forms of power, keep this world of ours in such a whirling turmoil that none of us has any time to climb off and examine the working parts. Certainly, in an earlier chapter, we were able to demonstrate how Big Monopoly Capitalism based in New York was busy financing Marxist revolution in

217

MAJOR C.H. DOUGLAS

Author of *"Economic Democracy"*
and founder of the Social Credit Movement.

Southern Africa, and since that is a thoroughly well documented story, it must count as an interesting pointer towards the money theories of Thomas Robertson and Major C.H. Douglas.

There are many hundreds of thousands of people in this country, millions perhaps, who are ready to appreciate the gruesome prospects that would face us if Soviet Communism enveloped the Western World. But how many have identified the other arm of the nutcracker? or having identified it, are brave and committed enough to measure up to the implications? Back along the road we met up with the capitalist lemming, a sober little chap so closely involved with his world of banking, investment and finance that he might remain totally blind to the evil propensities of the machine he helps to operate.

Well! the rest of us management-class capitalist-orientated citizens were also probably willing to offer up our uncritical approval until we caught this self-same apparatus processing blueprints for a collectivist revolution. After all, if you design a piece of equipment to manufacture, say, agricultural harvesters, and the business end of the conveyor belt starts spitting out swords, pangas and other instruments of death, then it's time to stop the works, monitor the moving parts, — and make drastic changes in the drawing office.

¶155.   THE MACHINE MINDERS

Ready by now to accept even one teeny-weeny bit of the argument? Or have you decided that it's all a bit of a giggle, — the product of a paranoic mind reared on the conspiratorial theory of history? Well confidentially we'd like to be able to agree with you. Many people who fully accept and understand *what* is happening, — who also endorse this volume's conclusions as to *why* it is happening, — are still unwilling to go along with the concept of a conscious conspiracy, — or series of interlinking conspiracies, — dominated by men of immense wealth and unbridled power. They find it easier to regard our whole socio-economic and political structure as a sort of complicated mechanism which has been put together on a piecemeal basis through the centuries, and which has developed its own creaks and inconsistencies, — aye, its tricks, its tantrums and its propensities for evil, — without most people being aware of it. On that hypothesis most of the lemming folk, and even a proportion of the lemming drovers, would have to be cast in the role of machine minders, running up and down the assembly line with oilcans and spanners, constantly checking belts, junctions and pressure gauges for fear that they will be made personally responsible for stopping the works, — yet seldom if ever being let into the secret of how the thing operates, and what will be the product at the end of the day.

O.k. Let's try it out on some recent episode of contemporary history. Let's *relate* to our own social and domestic situation, which is probably what concerns most people in the present context. And how better to do that than by examining the efforts to control inflation after the Thatcher Government came to power in May of 1979?

¶156.   MLR AS AN ENGINE OF
                          INFLATION

Inflation is perhaps the most unwelcome travelling companion of all who strive and yearn for a stable and prosperous society. Conservatives have more to fear from inflation than from almost any other economic circumstance. Well might the Fabian Arnold Toynbee proclaim it as an "engine of revolution", — *he* knew better than most the disruptive and disorientating effects of a rapid depreciation of the currency; how it bore most heavily upon the lowly paid, the pensioners and the fixed salary earners, the prudent and the thrifty, who by this means could be relieved of their savings just as effectively as if they had been mugged in a darkened alley. Inflation punishes the sober, continent and industrious, — benefits the speculative, the profligate and the spendthrift. Nothing is more detrimental to the traditions and the security of the state than a condition of perpetually changing values. Revolutionaries who set a premium on human misery may revel in the opportunity it offers, — but all manner of right-thinking honest folk have every reason to be appalled.

So far none of this is controversial. The thinking public was ready to support the new government in its counter-inflation measures, even if these should turn out to be temporarily unpleasant, and when Sir Geoffrey Howe raised the Minimum Lending Rate to 14% in the 1979 budget, the monetarists among us nodded their approval, opining wisely that a few months of this staggering impost would squeeze out the surplus money that was sloshing about in the system, and lower wage and salary expectations, particularly in the private sector of industry, as bank borrowing became more expensive. The measure was also reckoned to be a significant long-term factor in reducing the rate of inflation.

In mid-November, approximately six months later, by which time this monetarist device was originally expected to take effect, the Chancellor carried his policy a stage further by raising the MLR to an unprecedented 17%, on which basis bank lending for industry was running at 20%, with building society mortages some five points lower. The reason given for this incredibly high level of interest rates on borrowed capital was that, despite the previous measures and the prognostications to the contrary, bank lending had not decreased at all. In fact, in some perverse fashion, it just kept on rising.

¶157. PERVERSITY OF EXPANDED BORROWING
ON HIGH INTEREST RATES

Other things were also rising, — manufacturers' costs for instance, and retail and servicing prices, — and working men's wage expectations, — and local authority rate demands, — and when the reasons and the motives were analysed, a goodly proportion of the increases, proposed or otherwise, would be related back to the punitive costs of borrowing money. So the orthodox device which had been introduced as a means of curbing inflation was apparently pulling in a contrary direction. The dosage prescribed for treating the symptoms was simply inflaming the original disorder. Long-established economic theories went overboard as we discovered from bitter experience that inflation was merely keeping step with the rise in MLR.

So what had gone wrong with the conventional wisdom, which had dictated all through the Keynesian era that the way to take excess money out of the system was to raise taxes and interest rates? That might work if money was a finite entity that could be limited to banknotes and silver coin. But in point of fact the vast bulk of financial transactions in a sophisticated economy are done on credit. Raising the costs of obtaining credit does not necessarily reduce the amount of credit demanded, — merely intensifies the inflation spiral as producers amend their pricing structures to accommodate the higher borrowings. Up prices! Up wages! On goes the giddy merry-go-round.

As a result of this traumatic experience, had we stumbled therefore on a fundamental fallacy in orthodox financial thinking? Many years ago Major C.H. Douglas maintained that there was such a fallacy, and made a serious contention which has never been discounted or disproved. He argued that when money is withdrawn from the economic system by means of interest-bearing debit finance, it creates a shortfall between what the producers earn in wages and salaries, and the prices that they will collectively have to pay to buy back the end products of their combined efforts and ingenuity, — and that such a system can only be kept in a state of unstable equilibrium by depression, or inflation, or both.

The basic tenet of this contention was relatively unimportant when funds were freely available at rates in the region of five per cent, but with an MLR at seventeen, and ordinary commercial overdrafts mulcting the borrower of one-fifth of his loan capital on a year-to-year basis, one would have to be very sure of the utter infallibility of financial orthodoxy to will that this process should continue.

But after the inflationary surges of the seventies, how can we *be* so sure? Switzerland, West Germany and the United States, the three western developed nations who emerged most successfully from the 1973-74 oil price spiral, did so on relatively low interest rates. America only went into double-digit inflation during 1979-80, — by which time the Fed. had induced its domestic banking system to join the interest-rate hike. When the Germans and the Swiss also jacked up their lending rates so as not to be left completely behind in the usury stakes, their experience was exactly similar to what had happened in Britain, — their business men and industrialists developed such an insatiable demand for additional funds that the central banks felt obliged to screw the rates higher still as a discouragement to this illogical perversity.

¶158. THE EVIL OF TREATING MONEY AS A COMMODITY

It is all a case of deciding what came first between the chicken and the egg, — what was the cause and what was the effect. For sure, there are many factors which from time to time contribute to inflationary pressures, — and in recent years the most significant has been the surging price of oil. But oil is an essential commodity whose scarcity value has now been impressed upon the producers, most of whom have little else to offer, and are therefore postponing the day when their economies go back to the desert.

The inherent evil in our modern-day financial orthodoxies is that they have bemused our economists into treating money likewise, — as a commodity of finite supply and limited availability which in times of stress can command its own scarcity value. Money is no such thing. It is a universal unit of exchange which need only be limited by the human and material resources available to command its profitable utilisation. This is a truth which seems to have been obvious to the New England colonists who, according to Benjamin Franklin, issued their Colonial Scrip in proportion to the needs of their own trade and industry. We are told that when their status changed, and they were forced to *buy* their money from the Bank of England, they lost a great deal of their earlier prosperity, and there was depression and unemployment on the Atlantic seaboard.

When Rhodesia was subjected to mandatory trade and financial sanctions, and was therefore cut off from international money markets, she achieved an economic miracle which astonished the world, and which was moreover such an affront to the orthodox banking establishment that it could not be allowed to continue indefinitely. She achieved it on a bank rate which was never more than 6½%, and during the years of her isolation domestic costs were so well contained that at one time the Rhodesian dollar looked as though it might double in purchasing value against the pound sterling.

¶159.   FINANCIAL RECTITUDE AND
SOCIAL JUSTICE

In February of 1980 a Mr. Norman M. Chapman of London S.W.1 wrote to the *Sunday Telegraph* with what many financial orthodoxists must have regarded as a heretical proposal. Noting that the months of skyhigh interest rates had inflated the profits of the trading banks to an indecent £1500 million, he suggested that the Chancellor of the Exchequer should take back a substantial proportion of this windfall revenue by means of a special tax levy, thereby reducing the Government's borrowing requirement, or perhaps creating funds for deployment in other sections of the economy. Mr. Chapman did not spell out the harm that had been done to the country in the accumulation of this embarrassing and largely unwanted windfall, but as should be apparent from our earlier examples, it had contributed to surging prices, escalating wage demands, strikes, deepening depression and unemployment.

Was Douglas right after all? Had all this aggro, this growing sense of insecurity amongst ordinary working people, been caused by a widening of the shortfall between earnings and prices, — a shortfall which had been sharply aggravated by the steep rise in interest rates; and which not only contained the elements of social injustice, but also tended to erode the public's faith in the only philosophy which can save us from a collectivist future?

When a previous Conservative administration collapsed in disarray, it was generally reckoned to have happened because its Prime Minister failed to come to terms with the miners' strike of February 1974. But here again we have become confused between effects and causes. The background to that particular situation was an inflationary groundswell topped by a speculative property boom. Unchecked central government and local authority spending had brought the conventional response of high and higher interest rates, — which stoked up the inflation, — which in turn brought a rash of apparently immoderate wage demands from a working population that was seeing its living standards eroded for the benefit of all manner of high-flying financial institutions who had seldom had it so good.

¶160.   CONSERVATIVES AND THE
          FINANCIAL ESTABLISHMENT

We had not expected, had we, as we advanced through the later stages of the counter-revolution, that we would come upon such a glowering and threatening Castle Formidable? But there it is, with its keep and its battlements intact, looming against the skyline, — what many have regarded as a bastion of unassailable privilege.

Do we, as conservatives, now have the courage and the pertinacity to stop and invest this stronghold, demanding that it relinquish some of its illegitimate and monopoly power? Or do we slip quietly by, hoping that our passage will not be noticed, — that the lofty denizens will not be disturbed? And if we do indeed slip quietly by, — as generations of our like have done before us, — how do we know that its drawbridges will not be lowered at a psychological moment to assail our flanks and our rear with a host of bloody men-at-arms?

For is this not the most revealing message of *The Lemming Folk*, — that under assault from the depredators and many-sided manipulators, our society cannot survive on a base of rigidities of class, or privilege, — or financial structure? that in the light of what we have so recently learned, the conservative who loves his country and its unique and liberal institutions can no longer hope to protect them by nuzzling down defensively beside the monetary orthodoxies which for so long have been regarded as support pillars of the capitalist edifice? that by doing so he could conceivably meet a similar fate to the buck that shacks up with the leopard, or the pigeon that goes nesting with the falcon?

Specifically, for those who are a bit vague on imagery, that means creation of a situation in which surges and excesses of the monetary mechanism cause an unwarranted aggrandisement of the financial apparatus, at the expense of beneficial pro- duction, — and people's lives and living standards. Workers demonstrating in the streets! Disgruntled pickets hanging around factory gates! All manner of good honest folks, un- tutored in economics, knowing only that the value of their money is eroding in their pockets, and that the System is somehow failing to deliver even a modicum of their aspirations! Marxists, Socialist revolutionaries, agitators, *agents provocateurs* ready to exploit every seeming injustice, every grievance, — themselves totally dedicated to destruction of a Capital-Finance structure which they have always alleged to be the enemy of all working people! In the ultimate, a disaster for conservatism and the free society! But not for the finance-mechanism manipu- lators, who in the past have survived much more violent cataclysms, — who had been known to re-establish the principles and the procedures of orthodox finance whilst the tumbrils rolled, and the blood was still flowing in the gutters!

¶161.   AN ADMISSION FROM
                MILTON FRIEDMAN

So what can be done about it? Well, when we fight inflation, let's fight it with no holds barred, and no deliberate obfuscation of the fundamental truths, which are not so difficult to discover if we will but look and listen. There is an old Indian proverb which says that the way to cut down a tree *is to cut down a tree*, — presumably without simultaneously taking away a wide swath of the adjoining forest. Even the renowned Milton Friedman, when conducting some talks and discussions in London in the early months of 1980, conceded privately on one occasion that high interest rates were a "secondary" cause of inflation.

Surely that's enough! We have a state of *primary* inflation, so we employ a device which, — upon the significant admission of a famous monetary expert, — is a contributory factor of *secondary* inflation. The patient is anaemic, so we open his veins and bleed him. The fire is sullenly smouldering, so we open the door, blow in oxygen and fan the flames. Mercifully medicine and fire-fighting have both emerged from their mediaeval obscurity, but it would seem that for various reasons financial procedures remain deliberately unenlightened.

As conservatives we are agreed upon a return to individual rights and responsibilities; a slashing of state bureaucracy and its profligate expenditures; a restoration of competitiveness in private industry and commercial standards of efficiency for the public sector; balance of powers and bargaining as between management and labour; over all an elimination of waste and restrictiveness in our social and economic processes, so that our country and all its people get the very best out of the resources that are within our borders and around our coasts. Everything in fact for which Thatcherism has been justly acclaimed, and which can give such much needed hope to a dismayed and disorientated world!

But it may be that all these aspirations will be fleeting in realisation, or impossible of attainment, unless we detect and expose that fatal flaw in the monetarist creed which, over the centuries, has enburdened us with such a crazy debt structure that local authorities are using half of their rates revenue to service long-forgotten loans; and which more recently has thrown the trading banks a £1500 million windfall at a time when councils, nationalised corporations and private sector industry were jacking up the price inflation to pay the costs of ultra-expensive finance.

The way to cut down a tree, said the old Indian, *was to cut down a tree.* Let's do it that way, — without flattening the rest of the forest, — or exacerbating divisions within our society. There must be direct means of restricting credit and reducing money supply which are readily available to both Government and Treasury, and which do not aggravate the alienation of one section of the population from the other. According to

C.H. Douglas, — who on the threshold of the eighties shows signs of staging a posthumous revival, — the root cause of that alienation is the orthodox practice of drawing money out of the system by debit-financing, thereby creating a shortfall between the end product price of goods and services, and the total amount that is available in wages and salaries to pay for them. Douglas suggested that *one* way of making good this shortfall was the distribution of a national dividend, — and as we come closer to the robot revolution, with its prospects of a traumatic redeployment of human hands and skills, that is an idea which deserves more than a horse laugh from the high priests of orthodox finance. As we have seen with James Albus, it may in fact be the only means of dignifying and humanising the advent of computerised robot technology within the framework of a free enterprise capitalist society.

¶162.   THE TWO FACES OF
                      CAPITALISM

Capitalist? But do we still dare to promote and uphold capitalism after exposing how its association with the traditional finance structure has created areas of privilege and illegitimate power? Well! here we must avoid the classic mistake of throwing the baby out with the bath water, — must strive to make that crucial distinction as between the ploys of THE COMPANY and the legitimate wealth-creating activities of home and externally sponsored capitalist enterprises which, in the aggregate, have raised our expectations and our living standards beyond the wildest dreams of our not-too-distant ancestors.

The ground-roots capitalist structure, born out of a community's needs to develop its productive capacities for the common good, has both a heart and a conscience, and a unanimity of purpose with both the people it employs and the customers it serves. Ideally it remains fiercely loyal to its local or national base, and encourages the spread of prosperity in its hinterland by reciprocal trading round its own door. In postwar years some of the supra-national corporations have also managed to implant themselves into local complexes in the developed

THE LEMMING FOLK

world, and in addition to providing a welcome influx of technology, have exercised a conscience and a sense of social responsibility in the highest standards of community-based capitalism.

International Finance-Power Capitalism presents itself on the other hand as a sort of parasite which owes no loyalties to country, class or creed, knows no morality, no faith, no higher purpose but the accumulation of power and profit. When ex-Prime Minister Edward Heath spoke about capitalism's "unacceptable face", he was referring specifically to Lonrho, an internationally orientated investment group which has mushroomed out of the revolutionary turmoil of emergent Africa, and which many astute conspiracy watchers believe to be an instrument of globalist policy in that strategic area. Lonrho specialises in mergers and takeovers, — and by the recent acquisition of Scottish and Universal Investments, became proprietor of the Glasgow Herald. Whether this direct access to the mass media was calculated or incidental, we are not privileged to say, but it is at least intriguing to speculate how the change of ownership may have influenced the views and the outlook of Scotland's formerly independent national newspaper.

Sacks of the highly toxic sodium fluoride carelessly stored at a U.K. waterworks where fluoridation is in progress. One area in which the Thatcher Government has thus far failed to control the state bureaucracy. See pages 180 - 187.

CHAPTER EIGHTEEN

¶163. **Prospects of Turning the Lemming Tide**

So! where are we? And what have we achieved? For sure, you and I can do little to confront and neutralise the élitist operators of the Big Power game, but if we at least become aware of their objectives and their depredations, even at a humble individual level we can help to expose and nullify so many of their subversive agencies. If you think about it, you will realise that almost all the lemming folk are either unconscious dupes or paid servants of THE COMPANY in its wider and conspiratorial role as an instrument of monopolist and ultimately collectivist global power.

Within any nation there are submerged forces which run contrary to the national urge for betterment and increased well-being, — forces of lust and licence, of disloyalty and greed, of irrationality and subversion, of anarchy and lawlessness, and sheer downright perversity that has to be different whatever. In normal times, and under natural laws of averages and balances, the overall effect of the positive elements in society is sufficient comfortably to contain the discordant, the treacherous and the criminally perverted; so that it is not always of supreme national importance that the subtractors and the detractors should be catalogued and defined.

Unfortunately these are not normal times, — and natural laws of give and take, pro and con, *herefor* and *whyfor* are not being allowed that healthy interplay which provides a balanced

231

viewpoint on the things that matter most to our national survival. Too much of what passes for frank opinion is being slanted and controlled, and too often it is being slanted in the same direction. For many years now we have been subject to a conditioning process which is intended to erode our sense of tradition and ethnic identity, so that we might never again emerge as a proud and spirited people. Most of this conditioning is done through the various outlets of the media, in accordance with COMPANY policy. You might be surprised at the extent to which the Western World mass communications industry has already fallen under the influence, or the direct ownership, of THE COMPANY, and how much is still passing into their hands.

Our country, our society, is at war. It has been at war for some years now, without most of us being aware of it. The traditions, the institutions and the way of life which we hold most dear are almost continuously under assault, and if we do not make a positive and a concerted effort to defend them, they will ultimately disappear.

¶164.   VANTAGE POINTS IN
               THE THIRD WORLD WAR

This is what is meant by the Third World War, — that subtle, insidious, undeclared psychopolitical conflict which recognises no frontiers, no barriers of race or language or culture, — no treaties, no solemn pacts or observances, no customs, no traditions of morality and decency, no valour or self-sacrifice, — nothing but the obsessive urge to thrust the whole of humanity into a single conforming mould, out of which there can be no deviation, no enlargement of the human soul, no appreciation of the infinite, or of the mysteries of life and the hereafter, beyond what the ideologues themselves will have considered safe for the masses to swallow and regurgitate, as and when called upon to do so by global government decree.

One must accept that for those of us who are in the midst of it, this Third World War is physically a less rigorous experience than other conflicts we have known. It makes no apparent demands upon one's time, one's energies, or qualities of resolve or endurance. It does not thus far wrench husbands from wives, fathers from families, sons from the bosom of their parents. It does not call for blood sacrifices, or even a temporary diversion from one's business, hobbies or pastimes. It is a war that is being fought in the workshop and the factory, at the office desk, and relaxing in front of the television of an evening. It is a war of words and ideas, – and the West has been losing heavily in the initial stages of the contest; first of all because in the main it has failed to realise that a state of belligerency exists; and secondly because it is still psychologically divided as to the most effective way of holding its own ground.

As we have noted in our earlier skirmishes round the subject, the scope is global and all-embracing. It permeates our social and political attitudes and associations; music, art, literature, drama and the world of sport; commerce and inter-state diplomacy; journalism, broadcasting both sound and visual; education, ethnic values and characteristics, – all that plus the tangled relationships between men and women. All have come under attack without us being immediately aware of it, – all have been given a slant which has canted them in favour of the psychopolitical aggressor.

And what has been the principal vantage point seized by the enemy in this war of words and ideas up to the present time? Just this! the critical psychological advantage of having half-persuaded us that, come what might, the final victory will belong to him. All those who already believe this have become early casualties in the undeclared conflict, psychopolitical prisoners of war.

Some of those have slid meekly and unresistingly into this point of view because their lack of a religious faith or moral background has made them an easy target for the socialistic and egalitarian concepts which the Marxist-Fabian collectivists have held out as paramount priorities of their new social order. Others have been so inordinately impressed by the fantastic successes which the Soviets have already achieved in their drive towards world hegemony, that they have decided further

233

resistance would not only be useless, but likely to precipitate a nuclear war.

Without believing in collectivism themselves, they have therefore tacitly accepted all the implications of a collectivist and totalitarian future, — the dark and forbidding prospect of a bureaucratised tyranny which could be fastened upon the whole of humanity for a thousand years, since by the time it had come to pass, there would be no agency left on earth with sufficient power to resist or overturn it.

¶165. PSYCHOPOLITICS AND THE LEMMINGS

What about the rest of us, — those who have not yet joined the lemming rush into oblivion, and have thus retained to ourselves some freedom of independent thought and action? What do we really think of this Third World War, and of our prospects of turning the tide? Are we for instance just a little bit apprehensive that any form of determined counter-attack to psychopolitical subversion will evoke a furious and unpredictable reaction?

We should not be so concerned. The Soviets have indicated on more than one occasion that they have no particular incentive to attack an enemy who is ideologically and spiritually aware. Their instincts are to wait until moral turpitude and social and economic disintegration have so sapped the energies and the reactive impulses of the intended victim that he will eventually fall into their hands "like a ripe plum".

We are not going to stumble into that particular trap, are we? Surely not now! *We are not even going to cringe when the war drums are sounded in the wings, for that in itself is a tactic of psychopolitics.* Like a ripe plum, eh? Now we know that we *have* to stop giving ground in this armchair struggle of words and ideas, for there would be no question of us giving in without some kind of a fight, and if that took place when we were in a weakened state, we would be more likely to lose our all.

Conversely a successful resistance to the psychopolitical offensive could bring a veritable chain reaction of restored sanity and confidence, and thrust that dreaded nuclear con-frontation so much further into the background. It means, of course, doing something about the lemmings, that pathetic assortment of the fushionless, the over-credulous and the ideologically brainwashed, whose deleterious effects upon a besieged society we have tried to measure in this volume. The subject has not been exhaustively explored, so there is plenty of scope for further investigation into lemming types and mutants, and an occasional paper that could broaden the minds of our students of sociology. In the meantime why not lemming hunts as a pastime comparable to motorway jaunting, spotting flying saucers or doing the daily crossword in the London Times?

¶166.   INTERPOL AND THE POLICE STATE

A final word upon that police state bureaucracy which might just be clamped down over us all if we don't manage to deflect the lemming swarms from their last headlong rush to the precipice! A Sunday Telegraph report in December of 1979 noted that the National Police Computer at Hendon already had about three and a half million people documented in its data banks. In addition to recognised criminals, these included individuals wanted for questioning, as well as motorists con-victed of traffic offences. A separate listing of vehicle owners was also fed into the system from the licensing centre in Swansea.

The report was at pains to lay suspicions that this sophisti-cated police computer had links with information stored by other government agencies, and whilst the files had to be readily accessible to chief constables and other public servants actively engaged in the battle against crime, there were technological safeguards against tapping of the stored data by unauthorised outsiders. The one way in which this could be done was by corrupting police officials who operated the terminals, a possibility which became an accomplished fact when an executive of a London gambling casino was found to be supplying his establishment with the names of luxury car owners from information that had been illegally obtained, either out of Hendon or one of its local links.

All right! crime must be fought, and the police are entitled to the most sophisticated equipment that money can buy. But what about the wider abuses of privileged knowledge? Some years ago Mr. Arthur Lewis M.P. was told in a parliamentary answer that there was no question of the Hendon computer being linked, *through Interpol*, with other police computer systems abroad.

Interpol? that romantic conception of an international crime-busting syndicate which has kindled many a schoolboy's imagination! The unfailing intelligence eye that picks them out, whether they come from Zurich or Hong Kong, Manhattan or Montmartre, Soho or San Francisco! The amateur student of criminology *expects* that there should be such an interlinking, and who can doubt that in practice it does happen, — especially where serious crime is concerned? Technology has made it possible, and where the means is available, the need will ultimately be found.

So who should worry most? the private car owner of Birmingham or Bridlington, — or the jet-setting drug smuggler from Bangkok or Bangalore? Without an international police organisation, how could the international criminal be tracked down and apprehended? If Interpol did not already exist, it would most likely have to be established. Everyone knew that Interpol was a "fabled network of global gendarmes forever at war with the preying powerful of international crime."

¶167.   A FINAL WORD OF WARNING

But is it? In "The Secret World of Interpol", Omar V. Garrison, an American investigative journalist, paints a vastly different picture. He uses a United States court hearing, which took place shortly after Watergate, to show this international detective agency as more of a communications network engaged in the storage and dissemination of information about both criminals and non-criminals. He also quotes a U.S. Treasury source for confirmation that Interpol's Washington bureau has direct access to the FBI Crime Centre computer, which presumably means that whenever the latter feeds in data upon an American citizen, that information can be made available in many capitals abroad. Since Interpol has links with several states behind the Iron Curtain, the possibilities for illegitimate and undemocratic use of this information are obvious.

Warming to his subject, Garrison tells the tale how Interpol, which originated in Vienna, fell into the complete control of Hitler's Nazis during the German occupation of Europe, and was transferred with all its staff and files to Berlin, where it became part of the Gestapo surveillance network. Even when it was being reorganised after the war, it retained several individuals who had been associated with it as an instrument of Nazi oppression, and incredibly, he says, its president from 1968 to 1972 was Paul Dickopf, a former SS officer who had served under Reinhard Heydrich.

The point Garrison was anxious to establish is that Interpol is a veritable cuckoo, with no legal status and *no accountability* to any of the sovereign nations within whose borders it has access to the most sophisticated methods of data gathering upon the lives of ordinary citizens. It is in fact a global surveillance system in embryo, and only needs the appointment of a politically motivated directorate to make of it what Himmler did for the Greater German Reich, or Stalin and the KGB have done for the USSR.

With that gruesome prospect in mind, anyone still feel indulgent towards the lemmings?

BIBLIOGRAPHY

"Human Ecology" (The Science of Social Adjustment) by Dr. Thomas Robertson, William MacLellan (Embryo) Ltd. Glasgow.

"Energy or Extinction", by Sir Frederick Hoyle.

"Fabian Freeway" by Rose L. Martin, Western Islands Boston and Los Angeles.

"Kissinger on the Couch" by Phyllis Schlafly and Chester Ward, Arlington House, New Rochelle, N.Y. U.S.A.

"The Rockefeller File" by Gary Allen, '76 Press, Seal Beach, California, U.S.A.

"The Secret U.S. War against South Africa" by Aida Parker, "The Citizen", Johannesburg, South Africa.

"National Suicide" by Antony C. Sutton, Arlington House, New Rochelle, U.S.A.

"The War on Gold" by Antony C. Sutton, Arlington House, New Rochelle, U.S.A.

"The Mind Benders" by James Gibb Stuart, William MacLellan (Embryo) Ltd., Glasgow.

"People's Capitalism" (The Economics of the Robot Revolution) by James S. Albus, New World Books, College Park, Maryland, U.S.A.

"The Battle for Rhodesia" by Douglas Reed, Haum Press, Cape Town, South Africa.

"The Babylonian Woe" by David Astle, Box 282, Toronto, Ontario, Canada.

"The Secret World of Interpol" by Omar V. Garrison, William MacLellan (Embryo) Ltd., Glasgow.

INDEX OF PERSONS AND ORGANISATIONS

Albus, James S. Author of "Peoples' Capitalism" — 134, 135, 136, 137, 138, 140, 142, 228.

Allen, Gary. American journalist, author of "Rockefeller File" — 104, 105.

Americans for Democratic Action (A.D.A.) — 26, 92

"American Opinion". Journal of John Birch Society. — 76

Anti-Nazi League (A.N.L.) — 54, 55, 58, 59, 95

Astle, David. Author "Babylonian Woe" — 200

Barbarians. South African rugby touring side — 177

Barber, Anthony (now Lord Barber). Sponsored Tax Credit Scheme as Chancellor 1970-74 — 140, 142

Benn, Anthony Wedgwood. — 166

Bernhardt, Prince. Consort of Queen Juliana of the Netherlands. Chairman of Bilderberg Group. — 42, 152, 165

Bevan, Aneurin. British left-wing Socialist, Cabinet Minister in Attlee Government. — 70

Bilderberg Group, Bilderbergers — 42, 109, 152, 155, 163, 164, 165, 166, 167

Blount, P. Clavell. Long-time campaigner against artificial fluoridation of public water supplies. — 184, 185

Blumenthal, Michael. — 152

Blunt, Sir Anthony. British spy for Russia — 132, 133, 216

British Fabian Society — 34, 163

Brooks, Wilfred. Editor "Rhodesian Property and Finance" — 206, 207

Brown, Dr. Harold. Member of Trilateral Commission — 152

Brzezinski, Prof. — 152

Buchan, Norman. Scottish Socialist M.P. — 36

Burgess, Guy — 132, 133, 216

Burk, Dr. Dean. American bio-chemist who publicised fluoride-cancer link. — 182

Callaghan, James. British Fabian. Prime Minister 1976-79. — 75, 97, 171, 173, 191, 212

Campaign for Nuclear Disarmament (C.N.D.) — 68

Campbell, Billy Lee. — 154

Fairgrieve, Russell. Conservative M.P. and Scottish Office Minister Thatcher Government. — 184, 185, 187, 189
Ford, Gerald T. President U.S.A. 1974-76 — 104, 108, 111, 152
Franklin, Benjamin — 223
Fraser, Lord, of Allander — 69
Friedman, Milton. American monetarist. — 226
"Friends of the Earth". Conservationist organisation — 63, 65, 68, 77, 78
Frost, David. Satirical T.V. broadcaster. — 42

Gama, Vasco da. Portuguese seafarer and explorer — 210
Gamelin, General. French generalissimo at commencement of Second World War — 53
Garrison, Omar V. Author of "The Secret World of Interpol" — 236, 237
Gayre, Robert. Scottish ethnologist — 211
George, Lloyd. British Prime Minister during First World War — 174
Gladstone, Wm. Ewart. 19th century Liberal politician and Prime Minister — 174
Graham, Lord Angus. Former Duke of Montrose. Signatory to Rhodesian U.D.I. — 198
"Greenpeace." Conservationist campaign organisation — 66, 68, 77

Hain, Peter, Anti-apartheid campaigner — 178
Hart, Judith M.P. Now Dame Judith Hart. Left-wing British socialist and former Cabinet Minister — 68, 69, 77
Healey, Denis. British Fabian, Chancellor of the Exchequer 1974-79 — 109, 163
Heath, Edward. British Conservative Prime Minister 1970-74 — 42, 162, 164, 172, 229
Hiss, Alger. Highly placed American Communist. An architect of the U.N. Charter. — 40, 41, 165
Ho Chi Minh. Leader of Vietcong. Dictator of North Vietnam — 85
Hoar, Wm. P. American writer — 25
Home, Sir Alec. British Conservative statesman. Prime Minister 1962-64 — 41, 42
House, Ed. M. Early American Fabian. Inspired the creation of the C.F.R. — 108, 152

241

Howe, Sir Geoffrey. Chancellor of the Exchequer under Margaret Thatcher — 221

Hoyle, Sir Frederick. Author of "Energy or Extinction" — 62, 63, 64, 65, 67

International Olympic Sports Committee — 180
Interpol — 235, 236, 237

John Birch Society — 28, 30, 31, 32
Joseph, Sir Keith. British Conservative M.P. and Cabinet Minister — 25, 33
Juliana, Queen of the Netherlands — 104

Kennedy, Edward. U.S. Senator — 150, 155, 157, 158
Kennedy, John F. President U.S.A. 1960-63 — 31, 110, 119
Kennedy, Mrs. Joan. Wife of Senator Edward Kennedy — 157, 158
Kennedy, Mrs. Rose. Widow of banker Joseph Kennedy — 155
Keynes, John M. British Fabian and founder of Socialist economics — 33
Khmer Rouge. Cambodia's fanatical Marxists - 45, 83, 217
Kissinger, Dr. Henry. — 110, 111, 112, 148, 152, 203, 204
Kruschev, Nikita — 110

Lamont, Bishop Donal. — 101
Lance, Bert. Georgian banker who served as a funding agent for President Carter — 154, 155
Lawyers' Committee for Civil Rights under the Law — 92
Leiss, Amelie C. Name on Carnegie Peace Foundation's plan for an invasion of South Africa. — 117
Lenin, Russian revolutionary — 15
Lewis, Arthur M.P. Parliamentary question on Interpol — 236
Lonrho. International investment group — 229
Lovins, Amory B. Conservationist who advocates "soft energy" techniques — 63, 78, 80

MacArthur, General Doug. U.S. war hero, commanding in Pacific and Korea — 85
McCarthy, Senator Joseph. Chairman of Committee for un-American Activities — 26, 92, 165
McDiarmid, Hugh. Scottish poet — 130

243

244